T0195035

DIARY OF THE DECADES
(The art in dealing with anxiety and depression)

Judder Leinenbach

authorHOUSE®

AuthorHouse™
1663 Liberty Drive
Bloomington, IN 47403
www.authorhouse.com
Phone: 833-262-8899

Published by AuthorHouse 11/12/2020

ISBN: 978-1-6655-0710-3 (sc)
ISBN: 978-1-6655-0708-0 (hc)
ISBN: 978-1-6655-0709-7 (e)

Library of Congress Control Number: 2020922123

Print information available on the last page.

This book is printed on acid-free paper.

IN CLOSING

The beginning is the end & the end is the beginning

When I began writing this book it was to reflect the songs, I had written in the past 25 years. I am approaching 40 and the middle life crisis is real. I have looked back at old photos, posters, songs, and lyrics. I both rediscovered and introduced in this book many of my unknown past scribbles and journaling. I must say I revisited mentally an out of sorts angry depressed anxiety ridden teenager. It was a little confusing and sad to reread some of those old horror stories. As I dug deeper and reflected on what I had written I decided to just publish them all. I cannot vouge for the quality of writing, but the context was factual. I am not the best writer nor do I profess to be but the stories I wrote were real to me. We all experience good, bad, and indifferent emotions growing up. I see this now when I look at my 14-year-old son. He reminds me a little of myself as he struggles to get by. I am so super proud of my wife Courtney and three children (Zadyn, Lenix, Maven) for putting up with my ass old angry self. They have an unconditional love for a guy just trying to get by and make things better for them. I pushed many people away throughout life and weltered in my own misery for many years. So many could not see this from the outside as I put up a good front. You can smile all day long and say the things people want to hear. Sadly, you cannot fool yourself and the more you bury deep inside the more you grovel in despair. So, thank you for taking a trip down memory lane with me. If you enjoyed any of this music while growing up, then great. If you did not well its best you try to find MP3.com, Napster, Myspace, or Pirates bay 20 years ago additions. I know my bandmates and I put a lot of time in writing these tracks. Hours and hours spent in the garage, writing, laughing, loving, raw emotion.

DEAR COURTNEY,

I do not know where to begin and how we got here. As I sit in this room and do not recognize the person sitting next to me. We have had problems as all couple do since the very beginning. Communication, lack of trust, and lack of intimacy being right up at the top. However, the last couple of years it has continuously declined. The fake it until you make it philosophy does not work for me. I need a partner not a coparent. I know we love each other and our children. In March 2020 Covid 19 my world was completely torn apart when I found out when Zadyn struggled with his deep dark depression. I could not fathom why this world that we created for him was so terrible. Every day I try to make an attempt to understand where you guys are in this upside-down Universe. The next thing is I am not sure what has happened or what I have done to deserve the absence of you in my life. I walk on eggshells daily trying not to say or do anything to upset you. I am not a perfect person and have plenty of flaws, but I do genuinely care. I do try to talk to you about the way I feel, and you look away and shutdown. I get no feedback or response and it's as if I am talking to myself. This makes me insane trying to understand what went wrong, what I did, what I can do? The next 3-5 days are absolute silence between us and a week later it is as if the delicate conversation never took place. "CupCake" I still do not understand where you are at in my life. I know money does not solve problems, but I have tried to make you all as comfortable and stress free as possible. Your living in a personal hell I have created with nothing to get excited about or look forward to. I know part of it was so you could have alone time but I also thought it was so you could avoid the opportunity of my advances. I need touch, laughter, and love in my life. Everything is fine with you as long as I do not complain. I do not work the same way as you. I cannot bury it all down any more like I used to. I want you and the kids to be happy. I also want to be there for you, and I will always be here for our family. Our days are what we make them. Carpe Diem… If we look for the positives around us, we will be more positive. If we concentrate on what we do have then we see the glass half full. Its simple yet so difficult to understand. I want to be a Better man and look for the good in people, the good in present, and the good in myself. I want us to look forward to the future together and not dwell on the past. What has been done is done and what will be will be. Its not the things that happen to us in this crazy world but it is the way we react to them. Insanity is doing the same thing and expecting different results. I don't want to be a grumpy old man any longer. I want to be the foundation and support for us all. Together we stand and divided we fall. There will always be sour days but if life gives you lemons pour me a glass of lemonade.

Love,
Justin

FRIDAY BEFORE 40

So, I have been dreading the big 40 for as long as I can remember. Specifically, the past 10 months. I do not know why middle age feels so weird. Possible because we are currently in the middle of Covid19. A global pandemic has swept the world. Our nation and everyone in it is losing their minds. If you were relatively happy before this occurred your now depressed. If you were depressed before this happened your now suicidal. It is absolute chaos & crazy. So many companies have gone under and the only ones that seem to be surviving are ecommerce. Jeff Bezos is making an absolute killing in this time of uncertainty. Here nor there I am talking a step back and looking at my accomplishments and downfalls. I know I should see more positive and be proud of what I have done in 39 years. I have created some cool kiddos, ok music, terrible poems, several companies, and hopefully some everlasting memories. However, It is difficult to focus on the positives and instead look at what has not been done or what I still strive to do. I want to travel but it's a global pandemic and travel outside the US is banned. I want to do more hobbies, but I have made my self so busy that there is not actual time for myself. You would think in the 200 some pages I have wrote in this book I would have learned a lesson by now. Humans are funny creatures as we want what we cannot have, and we take advantage of what we do have. The grass is always greener, and water is always wet. I hope I can get my crap together at some point and find balance. Focus on the important things and strive to be a better person. I need to listen more and speak less. Listen to the earth humming around me and enjoy the fruits of my labor. Money is the root of all evil not so much. It makes things easier but not essentially better. The simple pleasures of life are what make it worth living. I hope you find your reason to live and dream your big city dream.

JUDDER ML

POST SHOULD THIS ARMOR FAIL

2013

QUICK TO BE RETIRED (MARCH 9, 2020)

Breathe in deeply
Holy ghosts and pleasant parodies
When with you I'm pleased as piss to drive around so happily
Lean far into me embrace the comfort of our own home
Without you dad your kids are fearing how they will ever grow old
Without you by our sides
Trucks crash and good people die
We are the suffering the fallen
Grace of god he has been taken

So quick too quick to be retired
It's like he never even had a chance
Impact on his body's he is shattered
With every piece of broken glass
Turned upside down in 2 seconds
It ripped the life out of his chest
So quick too quick to be retired
It's like he never even had a chance

Oh god why have you taken him from me
Do you Hear us dad?
Our hero's dead
Where have you gone
Hear us dad
Our hero's dead
Why have you gone

So quick too quick to be retired
It's like he never even had a chance
Impacts on his body's he is shattered
With every piece of broken glass
Turned upside down in 2 seconds
It ripped the life out of his chest
So quick too quick to be retired

It's like he never even had a chance

SO LONG ASTORIA

Bombs away you leave me dead
So, close your eyes and shut the door
Your world is just not fair
our relationship is slowly ending
and it's time for you and I to stop pretending
that were still in love
even though we make it through another day
your breath is shy your bills are paid
so long
so wrong to say I long for yesterday
but so wrong

and I will adore you
even though it makes no sense
I swore not to hurt you
Is it wrong to say So long?

Pushing me and your pulling me
I can feel my blood boil my heart is racing
Enough with this girl
Over its over its time to leave here

and I will adore you
even though it makes no sense
I swore not to hurt you
So long

And I have adored you even though it makes no sense

and I will adore you
even though it makes no sense
I swore not to hurt you
So long

LAY DOWN TO SUMMER

Lay down your mercy
Lay down your trust
Lay down your worries
Lay down you to us
Lay down your worries
Lay down to the ground
Lay down your worries
lay down to the clouds
lay down your worries
lay down to the floor
lay down your worries
lay down to the ground
lay down your worries
lay down to us

SLEEPERS (YOU SLEPT THROUGH THE DAY)

One day you will see things as they are
not all colors are grey
until then you can dream your big city dreams
but they are all produced and paid

this is life
this is love
this is why
this is wrong
you had us all along
You slept through the day
the years pass us by
you still don't realize what you have until times up and were gone
this is true my dear

I tried to explain the way I feel
but you turned me away
the truth is you only hear what you want to hear
your too stubborn to bend

this is life
this is love
this is why
this is wrong
you had us all along

You slept through the day
the years pass us by
you still don't realize what you have until times up and were gone
this is true my dear

this is communication
this is motivation
this is communication
this is motivation

DESTINATION UNKNOWN

This is my destination
I still don't know where to go
This is the part where you and I have it out
This is my destination a vacation covered in snow
This is the try where you and I have had enough

I have had enough of you
put it this way it's your way or hell breaks lose
so were casting stones
put it this way it is your way I don't have a choice
a choice

This is my destination
I still don't know where to go
This is the part where you and I have it out
This is my destination a vacation covered in snow
This is the try where you and I have had enough

I have had enough of you
we have had enough of this long ago
but I still don't know where to go
oh, to find a way
to go and fall asleep
trust me
This is my destination
I still don't know where to go
This is the part where you and I have it out

all this fussing and fighting
don't dare cross her
now the children are crying
this time your pushing me and pulling me
sometimes you think your better than me
but I think you are going crazy ha ha ha

This is my destination
I still don't know where to go
This is the part where you and I have it out
This is my destination a vacation covered in snow
This is the try where you and I have had enough

CAN WE JUST

So, tell me now is the part where you have realized
All your dreams and all your fears seem to be unending
Tear my heart out slicing up into my arteries
Open your ears and not your eyes you'll hear me say
it's your fault
and I opened the door to the unknown
I miss the way you light up the room its yours
And sacrifice everyone that proves you wrong

can we just blame it on them all?
I see the world for what it is as long as you care
can we just stay here in this moment?
because we both know that you cannot stomach that it's your fault

can we just let it go tonight?
Let it go for tonight
it seems to fit exactly right
can we just forget about the downside?
to everything and everyone you try to justify

can we just blame it on them all?
I see the world for what it is as long as you can
can we just stay here in this moment?
because we both know that you cannot stomach that it's your fault

SHOULD THIS ARMOR FAIL

THE END OF HEARTACHE

2013

KYLE RANDY ALEX
CORY JUDDER L.

FAIR-WEATHER FAN

You save face with a virgin smile
such a character waste
You save face with a virgin smile
such a character waste
deception is your game
it makes me feel as if nothings real
it's just another day
your friendship is ok
when weathers fair
you are there
but the rain pushes you away

you can see I did not try
I cannot say I'm surprised
your there for me
when its best for you
my fair weather friends
you can see I did not try
I cannot say I'm surprised
your there for me
when its best for you
my fair weather fans

all bets aside, all bets aside always
all bets aside, all bets aside always
all bets aside, all bets aside always
I tried

To let it go and push it far
Your pushing me away
I tried
To let it go and push it far
Your pushing me away

I cannot say I'm surprised
your there for me
when its best for you
my fair weather friend
you can see I did not try
I can't say I'm surprised
your there for me
when its best for you my fair-weather fan

TRUE FRIENDS STAB YOU IN THE FRONT

I am scared tonight
As I turn out the lights
I am still sore from it all
let us go
there I was staring back upon my self
cut myself
waiting for the day to turn to night
ladies and gentlemen
physicians report 25% of teens suffer from anxiety and depression
there scared
I am so scared sick and sadly sound alone in disposition
I realize that is what is left inside is just another battle to my existence
I am scared

and last but not least I'm not the enemy of you
leave us alone
I am the voice inside you
and last but not least I'm not the enemy of you
leave us alone
I am the voice inside you

There I was staring back up at myself
Waiting for the state of mind to change
Tonight, tonight tonight

and last but not least I'm not the enemy of you
leave us alone
I am the voice inside you
and last but not least I'm not the enemy of you
leave us alone
I am am the voice inside you

I am scared tonight
As I turn out the lights
I am still sore
I'm still sore from it all
I'm scared tonight
As I turn out the lights
I'm still sore
I'm still sore from it all
Tonight, tonight tonight
I'm scared tonight

THE PROMISES WE KNOW

War
1 2
want to want to break into you
ill rip away your life
life is nothing but our own strife
this is not love but a little love affair
this means I cannot live without you anymore
this is not something I can shut my brain off to
this is the broken man's war
war I am frustrated
war and I struggle
I do not know who you are anymore
so, stay on your side
do not step up to me
I have nothing left to say to lose here anymore

Cause not all those that sleep are the ones that dream
And not all those that sleep our praying
we are falling backwards into the promises we know
who do you favor more the fruit or the fate or the worms?

the fruit the worms
razors edge, raise the dead
razors edge, raise the dead
razors edge, raise the dead
our fallen soldiers
razors edge, raise the dead

our fallen soldiers
every time I die
every time I die
I die I sleep inside
a shallow grave
every time I die
I die I sleep inside
a shallow grave

Cause not all those that sleep are the ones that dream
And not all those that sleep our praying
we are falling backwards into the promises we know
who do you favor more the fruit or the fate or the worms?
the fruit the worms

LENIX

As water fills my lungs
this is nothing short of forgettable
forgettable
forgettable
I can keep your beating still were unforgettable
staying up another sleepless night again
I'm pacing through the hospital when the doctor walks in
I can keep your beating still
Still were unforgettable

tonight, I feel perfect I'm alive
I can keep your heart beating still
a miracle at work
Tonight, it's impossible to deny
I can keep your beating still
were unforgettable

were unforgettable
sunlight breathe into him you breathe life into his lungs
I can keep your beating still
were unforgettable

tonight, I feel perfect I'm alive
I can keep your heart beating still
a miracle at work
Tonight, it's impossible to deny
I can keep your beating still
were unforgettable

I can keep your heart beating still
Lenix Breathe your life in us

FRAMELESS PICTURE

Can we pretend for a second that this makes sense?
All good things must come to an end
are we getting somewhere now?
find the reasons why I dread your company
either way you'll try you get in my face
cry your eyes out still
your tears are blowing up the phonelines
your wide awake but still you can't see this
if I could ask you
if I could ask you now
are we getting somewhere now?
are we getting somewhere?
because we wish you did
innocent and begging for it
look at yourself in the mirror
with the looks that kill
are we getting somewhere now?
are we getting somewhere?

Now when all seems a mess
were dead inside
All good things must come to an end
are we getting somewhere now?
a picture frame of our mistakes
is left plain in sight
All good things must come to an end
are we getting somewhere now?

are we getting somewhere now?
are we getting somewhere all the way down?
are we getting somewhere now?
close your eyes because you are never going to see me
a plastic smile and the lipstick on your lips
close your eyes because you're never going to see it's all down from
here
trust

when all seems a waste
were dead inside
All good things must come to an end
are we getting somewhere now?
a picture frame of our remains
is left plain in sight
All good things must come to an end
are we getting somewhere now?
are we getting somewhere now?
are we getting somewhere now?

SHOULD THIS ARMOR FAIL

4 SONG EP

2012

DWAYNE H. PETE L. KYLE P. RANDY B. CASSIDY M. JUDDER L.

D.A.R.E.

They say suffering is not for the strong
I am leaving you and your bad faults
they say suffering strikes us before we fall
I am bleeding tunes on horizons
they say suffering will surely end us
I am free to choose between death and fashion
they say suffering will end us all
your hearts truly break inside us
your hearts truly break inside
this is not to point a finger
this is not to call you out
I cannot afford to fix this
what you bring is suffering
this is suffering, this is what consumes you
this is suffering, this is what we breed
misery loves its company or is this just what it seems
your hearts truly break inside us
misery loves its company or is it just what it seems
your hearts truly break inside us
weak end scars I'm trying so hard
weak end scars I can't control you
waking skies I'm trying so hard
breaking skies I can't control
your eyes close I believe I bleed
I have got to stake it all in stride though
your eyes close I believe I bleed

I've got to take my time though
my body burns and breaks and bleeds
I will give it to you if this is what you need
my body burns and breaks and bleeds
I've got to let go
my body burns and breaks and bleeds
I will give it to you if this is what you need
my body burns and breaks and bleeds
I've got to let go
breaking yourself until your dead
your dead your dead your something unsaid
ways to bleed your blood
breaking yourself until your dead
your dead your dead your something unsaid
ways to bleed your blood
breaking yourself until your dead
your dead your dead your something left unsaid

BLUEPRINT TO SELF DESTRUCTION

Philosophies of guys unknown
philosophers just think about
with everything you say
this is the anthem to sing out loud
I'm on the edge of losing control
With a little box you always scream about
I always come unglued
I will never surrender my faith
upon the burning body it will arise
you are on the opposite side
you always come unglued
we burn and waken for the demons of tonight
put your hands together
there is no place to hide
did we get your attention?
shut your mouth and wake up
let me complete myself
a heart attack commotion and cadence come
let our battle be our fourth fall
up on the cliffside edge I sink about
there has got to be a better way
a better way I say or

ill burn to ashes our saviors in the son
I say we burn forever
The time is right the time is now
burn to ashes our saviors yet to come
ill burn forever
the time is right the time we burn

a burning fire leads our way
still on the edge of losing control
apostle tongue speaks to me
I always come unglued

ill burn to ashes the saviors in the sun
I say burn the others
the time is right the time we burn

rest inside the flames
rest inside the flames

ill burn to ashes our saviors in the son
I say we burn forever
The time is right the time is now
burn to ashes our saviors yet to come
ill burn forever
the time is right the time we burn

rest inside the flames
rest inside the flames
rest inside the flames
rest inside the flames

THE NARCISSIST

Make yourself or make your bed
a quiet grave to sleep in
your hands are shaking your stomach churns
regrets start to fill our days
a haunted house a getaway
with truth and guidance
steer clear of our way
it's simple yet refined
a kid's gift to create

you came back and tried to fool me
but I fought through every trick
you're not innocent and I'm not like you
and I will shame myself through all of this
why so ignorant
why so ignorant
why so ignorant

starting the summer wrong
at least trigger fate
with a natural chest movement
a rise of the stakes we've paid
glass full or glass half empty
see me impress my friends
everything to everyone or at least we thought
til were all ashamed all condemned to sin
we're telling truth while telling lies sinking

take all my faith steal from me again
taking its toll your dead to me you pig
then something occurred to me
another game of hide and seek
im so tired of being it
you're so pretentious
then something occurred to me
another game of hide and seek
im so tired of being it
you're so pretentious
when the spotlights upon you
will you still pretend to hide?
your burning bridges
your burning wild
your burning bridges
your burning wild

LIVING THE DREAM

This is our time
this our dream
whoa my life is but a dream yeah
This is our time
this our dream

whoa my life is but a dream yeah

This is our time to separate the men from the minced meat
you left me here all alone now forgive me
we're taking two steps forward then one back
we're taking two steps forward then one back

whoa I would do lot to make this all on my own
even if it means shattering the pieces
whoa I would do my best to build it up on my own
broken as we build it up together
well shatter all the pieces

This is our time
this our dream
This is our time
It's the air we breathe
Whoa
Remember the start
the pieces we built into a heart
remember the shock

of breaking up
Remember the start
the pieces we built into a heart
remember the shock
we're breaking up

whoa I would do lot to make this all on my own
even if it means shattering the pieces
whoa I would do my best to build it up on my own
broken as we build it up together
shatter all the pieces

we're taking two steps forward then one back
we're taking two steps forward then one back

SHOULD THIS ARMOR FAIL

Progression Through Unlearning

2011

DWAYNE H. KYLE P.
PETE L. JUDDER L.

INTEGRITAS DIVIDED

our nations are burning
the flames of our unlearning
disasters and demons
awaken angels healing
my brothers, my sisters
reach out to every listener
the human in suffering
this world is drowning in the blood
so, climb faster out
here underneath our brothers keep
our hands design
hope is dwindling, your struggling
your seventeen

oh, you are the patron of resistance
you shame my name creating drama & lies

so close to leaning toward violence
distorted visions of unrest are x2
you make the choice my friend

oh, you are the patron of resistance
you shame my name creating drama & lies

oh, you are the reason for the distance
your quick to blame put your ego aside

PROGRESSION THROUGH UNLEARNING

your eyes stare up at me petrified
look into my soul

you will never count on me to salt your wounds
& help you when you fail
your insecurity rises up
I push you to the ground
come take a walk with me, grab my hand
help me heal myself, myself
what I'm psycho
there is no place in my head
the cycle continues
I'll break lovers' fate
what is died is born
the fate left unsaved
awaken the swine
awake left unscathed
vigilant and possibly
confusion
takes a hold and comforts me
breaking bad
letting go so silently
ripping out
every heart as it beats
you take a pill

to settle down and to sleep
take a drink
to wake me up and caffeinate
repeating on
the daily grind hypocrisy
genocide
is starting to sound good to me inside

your eyes stare up at me petrified
looking into my soul

breaking (x3)
the daily cycles I'm
breaking (x3)
the star & circles I'm

DARKNESS AS THE COLOR OF ROSE

waking the early deal
dark hours dark evenings
sunrise is not quite here
nor flowers nor feeling
working my life away
for power, prestige
my body's slow decay
for money to feed
and in between if we could smell the roses
these fake machines turning our hearts
oh, this is not what you what
it is the shelter you need
its providing for your family
oh, this is not what you want
this is what you need
a warm embrace from the weak
you are a slave to the system
slave to the system
I can't bring myself
to waste my child's life
when will someone see?
what this is doing to me
is this what I am is 60 hours & 60 weeks
oh, start again the fading sun embarks
these are the days that I miss with you the most

and in between if we could smell the roses
these fake machines turning our hearts
Yeah
I adore what I ignore
with new life is this what we have been waiting for
to start it over

ET EN BRUT(SPREADING LOVE LIKE CANCER)

Pursuit, Punish the perils'
Grip tooth torn out and tangled roots
Stitches sew up my festered wounds
White cells so callous and trivial
This is the end of it all

Pursuit the punishment
Torn out and tangled out of
I smoke my cigarettes
This is the end of it all
Love is Life Heaven sent

You will not rape me out of love
My smiles Permanent
This is the end of it all
This Is my Life
It could be worse
Suffer the Curse

Wait for me down below
Greet me as though we never slowed
Wait for me
Cancer the Earth
Cancer the Earth
Cancer the Earth

MY MIDDLE NAME
IS VIOLENCE

Lies
Surrender your hearts
Surrender Your Guns
Beneath The sky
You're not what you want
The Air you Breathe is your life
It's not that you won
You watch them bleed
Like scabs to flies
It's not that you won
You watch them bleed
Behind your lies
I wish it could have been someone like me
To toss you back
back flat across the chalkboard
This kid walks into the classroom
With a gun in his hand
Oh, the look on his face
Ill feeling wrong
stand up son now get your wind back
I wish it could be so much simpler
But then media would have much to talk about

Raise your fists up and put your head back down
Shots firing kids dropping to the ground
Push away
violence
Push away

WAITING TO EXHALE FOR THE BEACONS OF LIGHT

War, War
All the time
We Wait for the Beacons of Light
Wait for it, Wait for it
Frustrations
Frustrations brewing both sides
Dedication
Dedication to my mind
Determination
Determination doing what's right
Revolution
Revolution Bombs ignite
Fall back, pick up the piece's men
Stay on track whistles and cadence crew
Full attack! There is no one left to rescue you
Freedom Reign, put your guts before glory too
Wait! Wait! Wait!
Storming Beaches to Declare War on you
Turn around place six feet under
Put your face into a hole
Put your damn hands up

THE BLACK CANDLE MASS

Demo

2010

DUSTIN R. NATHAN L.
KRIS O. JUDDER L.

INCUR

What new sounds do you sing to your babies?
Oh, what mood should you really be in
today the day in color
The day I called is the day I cried
I go along just for the ride
again, seatbelt sunburn
What is that they say who decides who is crazy
Learn we all fall for suspects
Your too scared of falling behind
Burnt your wasting all my time
Two steps forward then 3 behind
How much longer
Who decides who should be left behind and alone?
Antisocial antimetaphysically incapable of feeling love
Oh, right here we are shining through
Are you one of them or really is it you?
I swore never again to trust beyond myself
I am sick here, lying, waiting, so impatiently
I feel like I'm already dead inside skinned heartedly
I'm still waiting for her, but no one shows to comfort me
The world moves on and I feel that I am lazy
I come across as insecure at times -needles in my heart
Forward progress
I'm making moves inch by inch by
Still I'm left miles from home wonder what left
What is that they say who decides who's crazy
I wait here longer
Youth in somber

KRISTAL KASKET

I awake sleep walking
I awaken
I awake sleep walking
in the dead of night
the skeletons remain
I toss and turn all throughout the night
its towards the dawn of day the maze of sight
I speak through the crow's unrest and dirt's desire
they stir amongst the streets where the unholy meet
blood in my dreams so it seems is bitterness
my work haunts my nights inner trials of no consequence
my heart races rapidly as I run from my apparent doom
but the evil only lurks closer touching quite soon
I fight with all my might, but my attempts are futile
the one thing I can't control is my mind

THE ENEMY

Believe In Me
I Unfold
I'm Your Disease
I Unfold
You Think You Try
You Think Its Right
Well I'll Vote For
What I Do not Care About
You Think Its Right
You Think Its Mind
I Can Never Control My Brain
I Face My Emotion
I Am the One
I Face Imposition
The Trial of Time
I Defy Your Devotion
To Evade or Deny
I Face My Captors
I Am the Enemy
The Enemy In Me Completes Me Fine
You Think You Try
You Think Its Right
Well I Do not Know
But Somethings Severely Wrong
You Thinks Its Right
You Think Its Time
Time to Take Control of Your Life

Whine, Separate, Alleviate, All the Hate
Gun in Hand
Laying on The Floor with A Gun And Pillow
Like the Deserts Without Snow Carry Me On
I Think You Try but Can't Deny the Endless Doors Define
You Think You Know but Can't Control the Everlasting Son Of Gold
Can't Hold Me Here but I Feel Confined
I Will Not Be Beat Myself Up till I'm Blind
The Inner Flame Burns Blue Behind the Shun
My Test Is to Confess The Hate I Have To Endure
A Minor Threat the Trial Is Set
I Must Express My Sins to The World
I Summon You Too Finally Decide
Is It Wrong or Is It Right?
We Dispute the Charges of A This Demented Mind
The Child Accosted Again from Inside
Bipolar It Seems or A Test Of Fate
The Cross Provokes Us All to Medicate
The Enemy In Me Completes Me Fine

THUMP

lay up
I am not the one the one whose paying
lay up
for the quiet kids do not shy now take it
lay up
the damage is done the walls are painted
lay up
pull the trigger pull the trigger pull the trigger now
pull the trigger pull the trigger pull the trigger pow
we all heard the pops from the neighbor's school
the days you had taken for granted you stupid fool
mistakes you have made have been made simple now
the cold steel sounds as the fire strikes pow
lead empowers the young and impressionable minds
hearts break, moms freak as the first responders decide
the time of death 10 minutes past the hour
runaway run away from the emotional pain shower
the rollercoaster teenagers battle uphill
you never belonged and you never will
you are the one they will always make fun of weirdo
pointing fingers and cracking jokes at the zero
this autumn day cannot be undone
the D-day to some who lost their sons

TONE DEF

OH, START AGAIN
THE FADING SUN EMBARKS
THESE ARE THE DAYS THAT I MISS WITH YOU THE MOST
AN OATH TO SERVE YOU BEST
YOU'RE THE ONE I WANT AND CAN'T IGNORE
THESE ARE THE TIMES THAT ARE NATIONS HEART WILL SPARK
SOLD AS I STARE AT YOU
AND YOU'RE THE ONE I WANT
THESE ARE THE DAYS THAT I MISS WITH YOU THE MOST
SOLD AS I STARE AT YOU
YOU'RE THE ONLY ONE I WANT
THESE ARE THE DAYS THAT MISS WITH YOU TONE DEF
LOOK HERE AT ME IM THE PERSON NOT QUITE SEEN
COLD AND COVERED IN A BLANKET MAN-MADE MACHINE
SOFT I UNFOLD MY EMOTIONS OFF THE TV SCREEN
I DREAM OF A ROMANCE NOVEL INVOLVING YOU AND ME
SOLD AS I STARE AT YOU
AND YOU'RE THE ONE I WANT
THESE ARE THE DAYS THAT I MISS WITH YOU THE MOST
SOLD AS I STARE AT YOU
YOU'RE THE ONLY ONE I WANT
THESE ARE THE DAYS THAT MISS WITH YOU TONE DEF
LOOK WHAT YOU'VE WHAT YOU'VE BECOME
EYES SHUT COLD CONTAGIOUS
LOST LOVE FOR THE TAKING
EYES SHUT COLD CONTAGIOUS
WHAT IS WHAT IS LOVE

SHALLOW

ITS GIVEN ME SOME TIME TO REST I FEEL AS THOUGH IM DRAINED
LAYING STILL AS WATER WAITS IVE BECOME INSANE
WHAT A WASTE, A VICTIM
BEGGING ME BEGGING FOR MORE
WHAT A SHAME
WERE THEIR SYMPTOMS
I FEEL SO I FEEL SO LOST
YOUR MAKING FRIENDS FALLING ASLEEP
I CANNOT STAY AWAKE
THE BITTER PILLS TASTE SO SWEET
I CANNOT BE SAVED
WHAT A WASTE, A VICTIM
BEGGING ME BEGGING FOR MORE
WHAT A SHAME
WERE THEIR SYMPTOMS
I FEEL SO I FEEL SO LOST
WHAT A WASTE THE VICTIMS
MAKE ME SICK AND IM TIRED
OF WATCHING MY FRIENDS DIE
THE CITY SPEAKS IN TOUNGUE AND CHEEK
I FEEL A WARM SWEEP
ALONG THE CURB OF BROTHERS KEEP
SWALLOW THE BLUE FLAME
YOU TAKE BLAST FROM ME
YOU TAKE A BLAST WITH ME
WHAT A WASTE
THAT WE KNOW NOT WHAT WE DO

PARA PARA

BELIEF IS A NEED, A SEED WE GROW TRANSPARENTLY
CONFUSION LEADS US ALL FROM A LIARS CHAIR
SOWN AND REAPED WE SEEP THROUGH VAST GALAXIES
COMPOUNDED DUST, DIRT, DIVIDES ALL MAN
SPEAK TO ME IN LANGUAGE, A SMILE, A SLIVER, A RATTLE
A REASON SO JUSTIFIED OR FALL RIGHT DOWN TO YOUR KNEES IM
YOUR SERPENTINE. ILL REST RIGHT HERE INSIDE THE FLAMES
THROUGH YOUR WAYS I
I HAVE NO SENSE OF ONES SELF CONTROL
THROUGH YOUR WAYS OH
YOUR SERPENTS GUIDE OUR WAY ON
CARRIE ME HOME
THROUGH THE FAITH OF SUCCESS AND BLOOD, THE DYING SEPTEMBER
ELEVEN WAS ONE OF US
I WATCHED FROM HOME AS THE BUILDINGS THEY BURNED THE
PEOPLE WERE FALLING THE ASHES SWELLED THE EARTH
SERPENTS AND GODS STRIKING AT ONCE, BULLETS AND BATTLES
POISON ALL OF US SO FALL RIGHT DOWN TO YOUR KNEES IM YOUR
SERPENTINE
I WANT TO WRITE SYMBOLS MEANINGS
THROUGH YOUR WAYS I
I HAVE NO SENSE OF ONES SELF CONTROL
THROUGH YOUR WAYS OH
YOUR SERPENTS GUIDE OUR WAY ON
CARRIE ME HOME
THROUGH YOUR WAYS I FALL

THE BITTERNESS BURNS IN ME
THROUGH YOUR WAYS
IM IN HELL AND I BURN
FALL RIGHT DOWN TO YOUR KNEES IM YOUR SERPENTINE

THE ENEMY

I am lost, I am found
I try, to be loud
What's in your throat well I don't know
I don't know and I don't care about
It's a long road that we have to go
I've seen you twitch A gentle itch
I face my emotions I am the one
I face my devotions trial of time
I face everyday decisions evade or deny
Either way I am the enemy
Lie to deny or comply fight or fly
I am lost, I am found
I try, to be loud
What's in your throat well I don't know
I don't know and I don't care about
It's a long road that we have to go
I've seen you twitch A gentle itch
I face my emotions I am the one
I face my devotions trial of time
I face everyday decisions evade or deny
the enemy
lying on floor
like a whore asking for more
let to rhythm of our soul
carry me home
lying on floor
like a whore asking for more

let to rhythm of our soul
carry me home
I face my emotions I am the one
I face my devotions trial of time
I face everyday decisions evade or deny
Either way I am the enemy
Lie to deny or comply fight or fly
The enemy is in me

TWITCH

Lay your hair down for forty weeks
I've been condescending you hoe
I'm what you can't avoid
I'm what you cannot resist
inability to face consequence
as your stomach churns
your tongue seems to twitch
the smell brings morning sickness
bitter cold wind
I see a way a way through all this pain
Layton fragments
Sealed underneath what has been both breathtaking
I see a way a way through all this pain
This is obvious what is pattern less
this is obvious what is bloods lament
I wait here for
for you to comprehend
I have no idea why god has taken
I cannot seem to recall
my memory ceases to exist
the day I was born I died in 6 minutes
no more wearing the clothes
the dark and depressed
just to bury umbilical cord
bitter cold wind
I see a way a way through all this pain
Layton fragments

Sealed underneath what has been both breathtaking
I see a way a way through all this pain
This is obvious what is pattern less
this is obvious what is bloods lament
wearing black gowns
all dark and depressed
dressed to bury this unborn child
the questions that are asked
why did it turn out this way?
addressing death, it its own way
bitter cold wind
I see a way a way through all this pain
Layton fragments
Sealed underneath what has been both breathtaking
I see a way a way through all this pain
This is obvious what is pattern less
this is obvious what is bloods lament

FACTORY RECALL

I don't think you get it
I am the plague you suffer
I don't think you'll make it
I'm in the way you fumble
I am the walls that crumble
we are so much better that no shame leads our march
I am the way I am the one
The power within you will cringe from the sun
still I don't think you get it
Out of pain recover
walk away and you'll see
these thieves swallow lives to save
I'm lying in a shallow grave with
pictures burning page by page
it is the diary of a rotting me within
I don't think you get it
Shatter the pill discover
I don't think you'll make it
Breaking off a piece of plaster dust of my sleeves with disaster
we are so much better those who think their right
I am the way I am the one
The ones who defend you will die from the front
Still I don't think you get it
Out of pain recover
walk away and you will see
these thieves swallow lives to save
I'm lying in a shallow grave with

pictures burning page by page
it is the diary of a rotting me within
with a burning grin you will crumble
revolutions are redefined
I don't think you get it

SEMI -AUTOMATIC SERENADE

Your world comes crashing down on you
The cold steel sends the fire strikes and light
the end of ache turns bitter black and blue
the end empowers the overly oppressed minds
lay up
I'm not the one the one who's saying
lay up
four quiet kids are shot and slain there
lay up
the damage is done the walls are painted
lay up
down ten seconds down
Pull the trigger
pull the trigger
pull the trigger now
Pull the trigger
pull the trigger
pull the trigger pow
why oh why oh why oh you
runaway run away from the trouble
I'm the center of attack it seems all the time
pull the trigger point and laugh I watch you stumble
your lay in blood now it's all too late to try
runaway run away from the trouble
I'm the center of attack yes, all the time

mistakes you've made have all but been so simple
your hearts break as the chamber ignites the light
Your world comes crashing down on you
The cold steel sounds and the students fall in line
They hesitate as they blast across the chalkboard
the silence smiles as I take lives
lay up
I'm not the one the one who's playing
lay up
four quiet kids are now shot I'm saying
lay up
the damage is done the walls are painted
lay up
down ten seconds down
Pull the trigger
pull the trigger
pull the trigger now
Pull the trigger
pull the trigger pull the trigger pow why

SHALLOW 2

It's given me some time to rest
I feel as though I'm so drained
laying still as water waits
and I've become insane

what a waste
what a victim
begging me begging me
no escape from these symptoms
I feel so
I feel so
So lost

Your making friends while falling asleep
I cannot stay awake
these bitter pills that taste so cheap
and I cannot be saved

what a waste
what a victim
begging me begging me
no escape from these symptoms
I feel so
I feel so
So lost
what a waste a victim
I'm sick and tired of watching friends die

the local's dose while mothers weep
its common yet so strange
the city speaks in tongue and cheek
and I feel this warm sweep
through my body along the curb
my brothers keep and bury your best mate

what a waste
what a victim
begging me begging me
no escape from these symptoms
I feel so
I feel so
So lost
what a waste a victim it makes me sick
I'm sick and tired of watching friends die

You take blast from me
You take blast for me
You take blast from me
You take blast for me
You take blast from me
You take blast for me

what a waste
who's the victim
begging me begging me
no escape from these symptoms
I feel so I feel so
You're a waste
a victim it makes me sick
I'm sick and tired of watching friends die

You take blast from me
You take blast for me
You take blast from me
You take blast for me

What a waste that we know not we do

PISSING HOUSE

Either Way You Live You Live with Suffering
Either Way You Live You Live with Suffering
Either Way You Live You Live with Suffering
Either Way You Live You Live with Suffering
Come Out To Hide Ill Find A Place Inside
You Realize That Its All Fake
Your Last Words Worth Less Than My First Breath
Your Name Is Left Behind The Timeless Maze
Its All The Same To Me Yet
I Still Try To Get Inside Your Head
Either Way You Live You Live with Suffering
Either Way You Live You Live with Suffering
Either Way You Live You Live with Suffering
Either Way You Live You Live with Suffering
Crawl To Confide Ill Find A Place Inside
You Realize That Its All Fake
Your Last Words Worth Less Than Another Perk
Lust Behind The Word Sick
The Sickness Prescribes
The Real Drug Was Executed
Your Penis Flops
Now Your Demented And Inadequate
With The Weight Of It All
I Carry So Much Stress On My Shoulders
With The Weight Of It All
With The Weight Of It All
I Try To Self-Medicate At The End I'm Back Where I Started

INCUR 2

What mood songs do you sing your babies
I'm not sure Today I come home today I lost today I cried
I go along just for the ride again I feel lost
What's that they say
who decides who's crazy?

Words we both sought but did not here
to scared
to fall back in love
how much longer
What we both lost here along the years
To scared
To fall back in love
How much longer
Will we continue waste here in our own skin?
two steps to walk out the door
how much longer will it hurt

I go alone although my mind is hazy
A small trip & I feel a little insecure at times in my heart
completely sore I'm moving inch by inch by
still I'm left miles from home
the widespread panic
what's that they say who decides who's crazy

Words we both sought but did not here
to scared

to fall back in love
how much longer
What we both lost here along the years
To scared
To fall back in love
How much longer
Will we continue waste here in our own skin?
too scared to live our own lives
how much longer will it hurt

Words we sought that were unsaid
To scared
to fall back in love
how much longer
What we won't say and wont here
To scared
To fall back in love
How much longer
Will we all waste here in our own skin
two more steps to walk out the door
how much longer

DEADWATER

7 SONG EP

2008

ERIC R. ADAM W. SHANE M. JUDDER L.

THE MAYAN PROPHECY

days die out dark design cycle earth human demise
to save ourselves we must reverse the end of time
biosphere mass destruction subsides
raise your fists up age of the fifth sun
demolition ending the atmosphere
26000 years ruin the process of life
look out below
look out below
2012 judgement
look out below
look out below 2012
look out below
raise awareness for the coming destruction
revelations upon our spirits will rise
nations under one god or heresy
conjunction of our neighboring galaxy
to save thyself from humanities cry
look out below
look out below
2012 judgement
look out below
look out below 2012
look out below
raise awareness for the coming destruction
hurricanes ravage seaside's and coastline
tornados torture the country's inside
December culminates the human demise

with planet x in the timeline
love the skyscrapers crashing
the minutes of a mechanic clock
the Mayan prophecy it's time for
raise your fists for the coming destruction
look out below
look out below
2012 judgement
look out below
look out below 2012
look out below
raise awareness for the coming destruction

BURDEN

CHILDREN SEEK ADMISSION
TO SENSE OF DECISION
RECELECT ON A MINOR THREAT
COMMERICAL DESOLATE ESSENTIAL
TO WAKE BUT DONT FORGET
MAKE UP BREAKUP OF WHATS CODESCENDING
PARENTS FORGETTING TO SET THE STAGE UP HILL
AVOID THE BALANCE IN A SELF CONTROL LOSS AMENDS
A TIME TO RUN AND HIDE BUT
THE VULTURES REPRESENT THE STAGE AND STILL
WHEN CAUGHT UP IN THE MIDDLE
I FEEL LIKE NOTHINGS SIMPLE
CUT THE ROPE OF THIS MOOD AND WHAT IS LEFT IS TEMPER MENTAL
CAUSE EVERYONE MUST DRIVE THIS ROAD ALONE
THERES NO END IN SIGHT SEARCHING TO FIND MY HOME
IM TRYING HARD HERE TO FORGET
SO I WONT EVER HAVE TO LIVE WITH THE REGRET
THE BURDENS THAT I CARRY ON MY OWN
CHILDREN SEEK ADMISSION TO A SENSE OF DECISION
RECELECT ON A MINOR THREAT
COMMERICAL DESOLATE ESSENTIAL
IF YOU ARE LOST RIGHT NOW
I CAN TRY TO EXPLAIN SOMEHOW
THAT COMMERCIAL GARBAGE FED TO THE KIDS LEAVES A SERIOUS
BAD TASTE IN MY MOUTH CHRISTMAS LISTS CUT TREES GIFTS
GIVEN TO PLEASE YOUR LACK OF ATTENTION
AND DID I MENTION THATWHEN YOU FEED YOUR KID TV

THAT ISNT RIGHT TO ME
SO WHAT I SAY IS WHAT YOU NEED TO LISTEN TO RIGHT NOW
CAUSE EVERYONE MUST DRIVE THIS ROAD ALONE
THERES NO END IN SIGHT SEARCHING TO FIND MY HOME
IM TRYING HARD HERE TO FORGET
SO I WONT EVER HAVE TO LIVE WITH THE REGRET
THE BURDENS THAT I CARRY ON MY OWN
SEPARATION OF OUR STRENGHTH
COME ON WEAKNESS INSTILL OUR OWN FAITH & HOPE
NON EXCEMPT OF YOUR SHAME AT FAULT
SEPARATION OF OUR STRENGHTHS
CAUSE EVERYONE MUST DRIVE THIS ROAD ALONE
THERES NO END IN SIGHT SEARCHING TO FIND MY HOME
IM TRYING HARD HERE TO FORGET
SO I WONT EVER HAVE TO LIVE WITH THE REGRET
THE BURDENS THAT I CARRY ON MY OWN
CAUSE EVERYONE MUST DRIVE THIS ROAD ALONE
THERES NO END IN SIGHT SEARCHING TO FIND MY HOME
IM TRYING HARD HERE TO FORGET
SO I WONT EVER HAVE TO LIVE WITH THE REGRET
THE BURDENS THAT I CARRY ON MY OWN

RAIN

Children seek admission
to a scent of decision
recollect on a minor threat
commercial desolate essential
to wake up don't forget
make up the breakup of
what condescending parents forgetting to set the stage uphill
avoid the balance in
self-control loss amends
a time run and hide but the vultures represent the stage and still
when caught up in the middle
I feel like nothings simple
cut the rope of your mood and what is left is temper mental
cause everyone must drive this road alone
there's no end in sight I'm searching to find my home
I'm trying hard here to forget
that I won't have to always live with regret
the burdens that I carry on my own
Children seek admission
to a scent of decision
recollect on a minor threat
commercial desolate essential
if you are lost right now
I can try to explain somehow
The commercial garbage fed to the kids leaves a sick taste in my mouth
Christmas lists as long as trees
Gifts given to please

your lack of attention and did I forget to mention that
you feed your kid tv and that is not right to me
so what you need to do is listen to is right here
cause everyone must drive this road alone
there is no end in sight I'm searching to find my home
I'm trying hard here to forget
that I won't have to always live with regret
the burdens that I carry on my own
separation of our strength
weakness instills our own fate
resolution for our sins
separation of our strength
cause everyone must drive this road alone
there is no end in sight I'm searching to find my home
I'm trying hard here to forget
that I won't have to always live with regret
the burdens that I carry on my own

THE RISE OF SPADES

who would have known that the?
the costs would outweigh all of the benefits
who would have thought that?
the teachers been teaching nothing to our kids
who would have known that the?
train would derail so close to the station
who would have sought?
all the answers associated with youth innocence

even flow
the rise of spades
well cut them off
create
armies march
were beaten sore
raise the flag
defend
even flow

who would have known that the?
car crash would claim both lives in the accident
who would have thought that a?
president would be so hell bent on bloodshed
who would have known that our?
countries would be so well known for violence
who would have sought?
all the reasons for acts of treason built up by Americans

even flow
the rise of spades
well cut them off
create
armies march
were beaten sore
raise the flag
defend
even flow

the rise of spades
well cut them off
create
armies march
were beaten sore
raise the flag
defend
even flow (the rise of spades)
even flow (the rise of spades)
even flow

BLEEDING

we have been through this before and
our world is slowly changing
we have talked about it all
but it seems our communications fading
we have been through this before
despite broken dreams mistaken
we have planned our whole life out
my best friend and my worst enemy
and all in all, it's the same
so, who will take the blame?
before it all I was me
free to be who I want to be
before it all I could see
cut deeply let the bleeding begin
these tears never end
let the bleeding begin
these scars never end
let the bleeding begin
we have been through this before and
our world is slowly changing
we've so much across the mountains
coastal strands and plains
your finger zig zags spin over my spine
up and scratch my waist
created a fantasy of you
our connection is controversy
and all in all, it's the same

so, who will take the blame?
before it all I was me
free to be who I want to be
before it all I could see
cut deeply let the bleeding begin
these tears never end
let the bleeding begin
these scars never end
let the bleeding begin
these tears never end (let the bleeding begin)
these tears never end (let the bleeding begin)
I've talked with you about this
flip the switch no sense of self control
before it all I was me
free to be who I want to be
before it all I could see
cut deeply let the bleeding begin
these tears never end
let the bleeding begin
these scars never end
let the bleeding begin

REIGN EXCUSES

ill self-destruct and die just to entertain
egocentric, is what your friends might say
I've locked emotions up inside shattered veins
spineless puppets were stringing along in dismay
I'm indeed what they say
when your alone, your absent mind
reign excuses down
I cannot conceive this
the struggle to defeat me reign excuses down
no point in screaming, hope is slowly sinking
reign excuses down
I cannot believe this
the industry of slit wrists reign excuses down
prisoners of beating when won't you take me home?
I come across as cold, but I restrain
from conceptions that self-pity has no gain
my stories have no end, but they delay
in conclusion, there is no truth in what I have to say
I'm indeed what they say
when your alone, your absent mind
what is wrong when I'm right
what to do shot down in flight
I decide rape your mind
the illusion of safety reign excuses down
I cannot conceive this
the struggle to defeat me reign excuses down
no point in screaming hope is slowly sinking

reign excuses down
I cannot believe this
the industry of slit wrists reign excuses down
prisoners of beating when won't you take me home?
when you decide mind's eye
has been forsaken
tears of a broken child
confide on shoulders safety
reign excuses down
I cannot conceive this
the struggle to defeat me reign excuses down
no point in screaming hope is slowly sinking
reign excuses down
I cannot believe this
the industry of slit wrists reign excuses down
prisoners of beating when won't you take me home?

ARTERIAL RAZOR

I'm driving speedball crazy
it's the story of the day
Sleeping opposite of empty
pill bottles crowd my way
I'm drinking hard and heavy
12 steps completed in my head
Jumping from the second story
Broke wrists and low back pain
Empower
Rolling zero to sixty
It's the means to an end
Sick and sweating immensely
I've lost track of my best friends
I'm drinking hard and heavy
Each day I run away
Punching walls bleeding profusely
A downward spiral my life's in shreds
Empower

Decide the motion of this knife
Decide the purpose of your life

This is comforting to me
My life's fading grey
Angels with dull razor blades
Guardians at the gate

This is comforting to me
22 is middle age
dying young and angry
stupid and underpaid
Empower

Decide the motion of this knife
Decide the purpose of your life

1 2 3 floor
Empower

REFLECTION

Staring back at my own reflection
Of whom I am and want to be
Of chaos and of disorder rise of postmodern deconstruction
Period application A
Separate your seat at the table
With a frail bedazzled look
a series of stares
bound indiscretion

in your reflection
your reflection
in your reflection, reflection

to my surprise it bears no opinion
Of whom I am and want to be
Lucrative and equally suspenseful
secrets locked up in my dark closet
in your end of operation game
set your sight above at the target
take aim at what went wrong
a series of failed attempts at confession

in your reflection
reflection
in your reflection, reflection

whoa
a symbol of my age
a symphony of stars align
in the mix of who I claim
I still can't face my own reflection
can't face my own
Staring back at my own reflection
Of whom I am and want to be
Of chaos and of disorder rise of postmodern deconstruction
Period application A
Separate your seat at the table
With a frail bedazzled look
a series of stares
bound indiscretion
these are the pieces
the final reflections of me

I NEARLY LOST YOU

Summer afternoons they fade away
When the letters from you are erased in grey
When I think of you, I'm ashamed to say
that my life without you it seems so plain

I nearly lost you there
I wait here froze the moments pass
I nearly lost you there
I wait here for the miracle

When I wake up falling for yesterday
I hold back those tears drowning them down insane
Keeping all your secrets there locked away
I'm knowing in your heart its not ok

I nearly lost you there
I wait here froze the moments pass
I nearly lost you there
I wait here for the miracle

the miracle
miracle yeah
a miracle
a miracle
a miracle yeah

I'm a heartless soul I heard you cry
Sometimes I sit and just wonder why
I can't be everything people expect me to be
I guess I'm just callous but hey That is me

I nearly lost you there
I wait here froze the moments pass
I nearly lost you there
I wait here for the miracle

JUDDERML

365 DAYS OF SILENCE

2007

APPALACHIAN CHALET

The beauty of mountains
The loneliness of cold
Payphone call to friends
The yearning for control
In lapse of what we're seeking
In virtue we desire
These thoughts of repetition
Weaken our fire
The pain in times of need
The strength without the struggle
Flowers brighten her evenings
The color and role
Shaping plans for all of us
Mysteries one by one
The plot has been mistaken
For the enemy is your own

TRANSITION TO SOUND

Oh, it's what you can't do
it's what you can't see
insult and injure us all
I'm sitting on the outside looking at me
I'm taken by storm from the flood
Yeah where were you
taken to a safe place
my love where are you
where are you now
where are you going
where have you been
there's something not right
I miss you right now
I'll hold your soul true
I will to

WHERE ARE YOU NOW?

The stone and the silence
the memories of you in grey
the land of the free midsummer
the heads we turned along the way
the water washes away
at everything on its shores

Where were you
when I was down
where are you now

when you were miles abroad
I picked my telephone
I dialed 18754321
when it was dark in your hallway
I pointed my light towards you

Where were you
when I was down
where are you now
now

running on the way across the fields
when the leaves blow, I can see you
I can see you
See you, you

The last chorus screams as
my angst spills out onto my notebook
I write to you

Where were you
when I was down
where are you now
now, now

WAITING

I've whispered I've wondered
hold me today
I've been here I've longed for
someone to blame

I've waited for
I've waited for the ocean
I've waited for
I've waited for the ocean

The sand field the sum of
scratched again beneath
its twisted it's turned up
crawling away

I've waited for
I've waited for the ocean
I've waited for
I've waited for the ocean

I whispered that I was waiting for you

OCEANS & MIRRORS

The battle of matchsticks and man
To walk the line to kick a can

do not see
what's new to me
do not hear
oceans and mirrors
oceans and mirrors
oceans and mirrors

to tumble across the rocks and salt
I've seen them all and it its false
sense of your self
approaching the wind, the desert the sun

do not see
what's new to me
do not hear
oceans and mirrors

do not see
what's new to me
I'm not here
oceans and mirrors
oceans and mirrors
oceans and mirrors
oceans and mirrors
oceans and mirrors

CRADLE TO THE GRAVE

All the things you do not hear
I know you cannot see
Why must you seem so deaf
You are blind to me
So now I must go and release you from this sleepy cage
You were not the answer that I sought
or searched to need today
I start to feel the emptiness &

It's been too long without you by my side
I pray that I may heal myself before the grave
I've been so wrong to criticize your way

I guess we had nothing here
it's become so clear to me
now that your gone and my head is clear
it's my turn to walk away
it won't be hard to go away or so I have thought
I start to feel the emptiness and I know that I was wrong

It's been too long without you by my side
I pray that I may heal myself before the grave
I've been so wrong to criticize your way

All the secrets that you keep
you know we've been here before
being satisfied is my only choice

hanging on every word at your door
you have to say the emptiness has no place to stay

I've been so wrong to criticize your way
It's been too long without you by my side
I pray that I may heal myself before the grave
I've been so wrong to criticize your way

EVERYTHING SEEMS

I've seen you all torn apart
like the picture thrown from the wall
a piece of plaster remains intact
from what you could not fold
these are better days
that I wish to you

when everything seems to fail
that's when I appear
when everything seems to frail
that's when I appear

it seems to fail
seems to frail
my scrapes bleed across the pavement
the fractures that you've left in me
splinters remain in skin
infected by the times we've sinned
these are better days
that I wish for you

when everything seems to fail
that's when I appear
when everything seems
that's when I appear

I appear whole

AMBIONICZ

who knew we would reach the cross?
our lord we speak for him
and I will arise to bring truth on

we're fading out faster still
our youth can bring fullness to his will
and I will arise fate instilled
my will obeys him still

instilled upon the vacant skies
the memories of crying sons' eyes
opaque views from men of the land
crystal clear is faiths hand

we're fading out faster still
our youth can bring fullness to his will
and I will arise fate instilled
my will obeys him still

his will
I will

MY RED SKY

the red sky burns

the red sky burns

THE PUNK JAZZ

so easily to move on
I've said it before a catch twenty-two
I've grown up a bit how are you
I'm feeling old at twenty-six
I've done my time I've got my kicks
I've heard stories about the bird
and all the good music that can be heard
I don't what else I should say
to get my word out to you people today
we can move on

you know soon I'll be gone
as soon as my stories drawn
through words and tv
I'll be gone
through words and tv
I'll live on

ha, ha, ha, you know I wrote this huh
we've been through this song once before
I've been down my face in the floor
we've drank so much we got really sick
our high school years finding our niche
I've told you a lot about myself
I'd like to tell you all about my friends
but being how this is my story to give
talking about other people right now
doesn't make sense

you know soon I'll be gone
as soon as my stories drawn
through words and tv
I'll be gone
through words and tv
I'll live on

MISERY LOVES COMPANY

why she, she told me
that life is just a series of tragedies
why she, she taught me
the art of writing in sympathy

then why, why
vanity and wealth
a means to an end as well
vanity and wealth
misery loves company
misery loves me
misery loves company

there is beauty
with age it dies so slowly
where is the loyalty and sacrifice?
her misery loves a little company
simple modesty and calculated deception
the pursuit, the pursuit of happiness

then why, why
vanity and wealth
a means to an end as well
vanity and wealth
misery loves company
misery loves me
misery loves company

THE WEIGHT OF SPACE

wake up, wake up, wake up
the weight of sleeping
our breathing in unison
frigid air blocked by warm blankets
body heat circulating under the cotton cover
a stress-free zone of unexpected dream lapses
the anticipated arrival where my last episode left off
how fast the day is done
carpe diem
how a decade comes to pass
carpe diem
please enjoy while it lasts
fractions, fractions, fractions
portions of a day
fractions, fractions, fractions,
how quickly times a waste
from 16 to 64 almost overnight
10 hours of work times 5 days a week
52 weeks minus 365 days equals zero
the burden at hand is me versus me
wake up, wake up, wake up
the weight of sleeping
is lifted heaven scent
when I
when I wake up
I celebrate waking next to you
waking next to you

PRAY I

all the screams that you don't hear
but I know you can see
why must it seem so deaf and blind
use one of five senses to communicate need
can I still not see

the boy prays
he may heal
I pray I

heal my wounds
before my grave
fear the unforeseen
it has become so clear
my senses keen
other people walk beneath me
then why can you still not see

the boy prays
he may heal
I pray I

when I pray
that I may heal
I pray I

heal myself before it's too late
I'm so sorry I've criticized your faith
all the secrets you have forced on me
you saved this soul completely

DANCE U.S.A.

I wonder what I should do
to make a big difference to you
certain changes are most evident
in our near future
our times of unrest
home
it holds me close
my home
I could spend the rest of my life
indisposed, and enclosed,
reach over and take my hand
walk me home
my home is near
my home is with you dear

BELIEVE IT OR NOT

believe it or not I'm happy
despite the crazy things I write
believe it or not I'm happy
despite ambitions out of sight
to the things that I want
to the things that I need
dwindling in the light

believe it or not I'm happy
gods greatest gift of life
the whining of children
the silence of shame
the barks louder than the bite
the stress of not knowing if I can afford
the change for my next meal
utilities, rent, gas to go
the morning commute behind the wheel
the swelling of my joints
the cost of my cure
the American dreams for real

believe it or not I'm happy
to have my love in my arms
the air in my lungs
an audience appeal
a pen that works
to capture what is real

THE CERTAINTY

the certainty of simple
the solitude of heart
telephone to friends
to tell them what you're not
lack of self-control
a lapse of what is reason
in virtue I desire
soft and not satire
thoughts of repetition
weakening my mind
self-support in disposition
strength without struggle
flowers brighten evenings
their color and their role
shaping plans for all of us
mysterious one by one
the plot has been mistaken
you must pay the toll
I'm absolutely certain
that I'm not certain at all
a lapse of what is reason
for the enemy is your own

TO HAVE AND TO HOLD

This story begins on a mild august day
it's the story of an insecure boy
he has a frail and tender way
in the dark as to what might come
moment to moment he lived
always sedated and quite dumb
mother said Justin you need to have a little hope
in one ear and out the other
such a foolish immature dope
no promise for his future
only regrets from the past
how long will I live?
how long will this last?
then one day out of the blue
came a young girl who was insecure too
she was bold, she was brave
she was beautiful in shade
I've met this girl before
how could I forget her name?
she held me near when my skin turned cold
she is the best woman to have and to hold
it's hard to forgive and seek truth above
it's impossible to deny that this is love
the girl of my dreams please be true
continue to love me
and I will continue to love you

CENTER OF DECAY

it's been a long time
dealing with dismay
constant problems, future events
evidence of decay
unforgiving the latest trial
to break the family's cycle
there is little progress and nothing to show

forever in denial
walk past the obvious
ignore the written signs
this work is not of this world
forever in denial

the plague of uncertainty
the epitome of innocence
the first chapter of the heart
written with bloody hands
the flashy bracelet falling off
the secret to your success
the racing car on the backroad
that winds to so many teen deaths

walk past the obvious
ignore the written signs
this work is not of this world
forever in denial

ECHO

trust you said
the echoing voices in my head
stale, still, sucked of life
the dull edges of this knife
cut the fruit into pieces
such a sad pathetic lonely species
frail, bedazzled, little man
set apart by a strong hand
to throw a punch or save a life
to stumble the sand of deserts night
to the humble unrest
healing scars of the wrist
the changing weather to the soul
emotionally out of control
the early sunset commotion
set the future into full motion
the culture shock roller coaster
curving through generation x,,y,,z
publicized for all to see
the competing networks of your tv
perhaps it's a little flaky
the next big reality series
pilot renegade of unused celebrity
overdosed star power calamity
laying in the emergency room
overwhelmed by health care cost consume

American values are overdue
the cubicle you claim owes you
time oh time just wastes away
we are overworked and underpaid

SIGN OF THE TIMES

It's the sign of the times
ha
It's the sign of the times
Check it
It's the sign of the times
the sign of the times
if there's no reason then why
It's the sign of the times
I said check it
I woke up on the wrong side of the bed today
To much getting in my way
My face is faded
4Fit is coming straight from the underground
the sign of the times
check it you fisted motherfuckers
It's the sign of the times
the sign of the times
if there's no reason then why
the sign of the times
when there's no reason rhyme
the sign of the times
It's the sign of the times
if there's no reason then why
rock n roll yeah

JUDDERML

SOLITUDE OF HEART

2005

HOME AWAY FROM HOME

Alone and dreaming
For a place to grow
Your pointing your finger
A star given to me to show
That all is it forsaken
The search to feel at home
To feel at home
Home is where I stay
Home is everything to me
I wish you felt the same
We were once both on the same page
We have been through this before
we have seen this all again why we have to fight to win
we have seen this all before
we are repeating ourselves again
why we lost the chance to win
home my home
a fine place to stay
home my home
my hearts tender way
home my home
4 walls of love remain
We have been through this before
we have seen this all again

why must we have fight to win
we have seen this all before
we are repeating ourselves again
why we lost the chance to win

THE WINDING

the stains on the open floor
I hate some more and then I realize
that I might need help
I'm looking towards the dirty shore
I hate some more and then I realize
that once again I'm by myself

what has been done is done
and there is no way out
this shot's taken for my pain
as you scream and shout
what has been done is done
and there is no way out
what has been done is done
and there is no way out

there is no way out
there is one way out
were in winding
as were winding down the open road
I turn to left and then I drink some more
I said I drink some more and then I drink some more
and then I drink some more its sick

what has been done is done
and there is no way out
this shot's taken for my pain

as you scream and shout
what has been done is done
and there is no way out
what has been done is done
and there is no way out

TRUTH

you take away
you take away

I wish you could communicate safely
take a calm, cool, mid-range tone
if only you would speak soft and clearly
this angry language I really can't condone
words have two meanings when there said
your spoken lies I can't comprehend
your actions don't make sense to me at all

you take away
you take away

when I look into your eyes
I do not feel your true anymore
when I feel your tender skin
I am ashamed of what is with in
lies, deception, tainted thoughts fly
I do not deny it or question why
words have two meanings when there said
your spoken lies I can't comprehend
your actions don't make sense to me at all
words have two meanings with you
the words you speak
they aren't the truth

UNTITLED AGAIN

at first everything felt so right
but now it seems that I am unsure
if what it takes for you to smile
is for me to submit to your rule
have you ever felt this way before?

to see you again
to make you my friend
again, start again

the confusion takes on its toll
while we are waiting unhappily
for one another to be bold
and take the next step and just leave
it is so hard to leave
why don't I leave

to see you again
to make you my friend
again, we can start again

to see you again
to make you my friend
again, again

SPEAK FREE

if it at first you don't succeed then try again
lately I've been faced with a sickness betrayal of a friend
the remains of us lay shattered bound on broken glass
I moved to the south to try something new
who would of though my emotions grew blue?

speak freely
then you will see
that I was there
were you there for me?

I moved to the west to see what it held
I was amazed by the skylines, the mountains they sailed
the open miles seemed so surreal and untrue
I was torn on what I should do
it's sad but my heart wasn't there

speak freely
then you will see
that I was there
were you there for me?

speak freely
then you will see
that I was there

speak freely
then you will see
that I was there
were you there for me?
were you there for me?

WHY AM I SO TIRED

I'm tired of waiting
waiting this time
I'm tired of reading
your wrong when I'm right
when your face looks down on me
it portrays this sadness all the time
your face is filled with these unclean thoughts
sad, sick dim eyes

it's not the end of the world girl
just a slight delay at best
you worry too much darling
your brain needs a rest

I am sick of waiting for you to smile and say hello
yes, I am sick of you and all your problems
you mistake every word that I say
then somehow turn it against me in an evil way

it's not the end of the world girl
just a slight delay at best
you worry too much darling
your brain needs a rest

I am not going to stand for this demeanor anymore
anymore not anymore
sick, sad, faces without smiles
would it kill you just to smile?

RIGHT 55

I'm spent from another hard day at work
I drive right fifty-five to this irate household
what can I do just tell me what am I supposed to do?

I said hey
if you don't care then I don't mind
you don't have to worry about me
when you don't care then I don't mind
it's simple living in apathy
apathy

fighting depression at both ends
sometimes its silent
when the dark side attempts
to pull us apart
last week I decided to go out again
low and behold id run into someone I know
we caught up in old stories and rhymes
I couldn't believe the things we used to get into
ha, another great old time
telling once upon stories
back in the day

I said hey
if you don't care then I don't mind
you don't have to worry about me
when you don't care then I don't mind
it's simple living in apathy
apathy

RACECAR MADNESS

hey Jerry
my racecar is faster than yours

when we race against the time I win
when we race against father time I win
passing in the outside lane with turn signals on

when we race against the time I win
when we race against father time I win

I'm moving towards the inside lane
flying past the speed of light
my car takes the upcoming curve
with impossible fright
your car is in shambles
when it hits the side
the wall creates a binding
people are scared metals flying
I'm hurt, I'm crying
I feel like I'm the one dying
my heart is about to explode

when we race against the time I win
when we race against father time I win

PAGES

if you've read a book
then you've read them all
my stories tell of times
page by page
like when your wishing upon a star
do you really know who you are?

why
why must you be wrong
oh why
why must you be wrong
I'm wrong

I'm trying to reach the audience
I'm my own familiar way
touching your emotions
is my goal today

why
why don't you sing along?
oh why
why can't you sing my songs?
I'm wrong

you see I went to college at a two-year school
I learned so much that I didn't know what to do
rewind nine years
I feel I am a smarter man
a smarter man for writing this for you

DICOLE

I'm with a girl
she is a sight to see
a five-foot two emotional mystery
whenever I'm down
she's down with me

she is number one
a cold, cold northern breeze
bringing me down to my knees you see
she is number one
a cold, cold northern breeze
bringing me down to my knees you see

when I met her
I was lost as a man can be
she took me inside to warm my heart
we've built a love so strong
it can't be torn apart

she is number one
a cold, cold northern breeze
bringing me down to my knees you see
she is number one
a cold, cold northern breeze
bringing me down to my knees you see

and now you see

she is number one
a cold, cold northern breeze
bringing me down to my knees you see
she is number one
a cold, cold northern breeze
bringing me down to my knees you see

TREAZUN

DEMOS FROM THE BASEMENT

2003

Jason, Gabe, Ryan, Judder L.

DROWN IN SORROW

sidewalks and torn up streets
we tend to ignore the obvious
through longshots & desperate defeat
we're strangling away all of our hope
of good company and shaping words into poetry
imagination the possibility of no remorse

the same old routine of being sore
the same old
why can't you see that the rivers are overflowing?
we're drowning in our own sorrow
why can't you see that the rivers are overflowing?
we're drowning in our own sorrow

life is filled with tragedy
we tend to ignore all the obscene
cold sores and scratched up knees
the charity for all the poor
pursuit of modesty and shaping words into poetry
just imagine the possibility of no divorce

the same old routine of being sore
the same old
why can't you see that the rivers are overflowing?
we're drowning in our own sorrow
why can't you see that the rivers are overflowing?
we're drowning in our own sorrow

sidewalks and torn up streets
we tend to ignore the obvious
through longshots & desperate defeat
we're strangling away all of our hope
of humble modesty
try shaping words into poetry
imagination the possibility of no remorse
the same old routine of being sore
the same old
why can't you see that the rivers are overflowing?
we're drowning in our own sorrow
why can't you see that the rivers are overflowing?
we're drowning in our own sorrow
we're drowning
drown in sorrow
we're drowning
drown in sorrow

THE MEANS TO AN END

angst ridden youth follow in now one by one
we laid our heads down each day with the rising sun
i can count on you now more than just about anyone
or so i thought before the truth came crashing down on me
your telling my secrets while spreading so many lies
why can't you remember how we were last December?

it's a means to an end
the seven years we spent before
with exception to the good times shared
your still my backstabbing best friend next door
and I don't mind

who would have known that we end up casting stones?
tearing each other down and the bonds are childhood had formed
because your telling my secrets while spreading all those lies
why can't you remember how we were last December?

it's a means to an end
the seven years we spent before
with exception to the good times shared
your still my backstabbing best friend next door
and I don't mind

Yeah
was it worth it to betray all of my trust?
was it worth it to degrade our love?

it's a means to an end
the seven years we spent before
with exception to the good times shared
your still my backstabbing best friend next door
and I don't mind

looking back
what are we fighting for?

BAR FLY

our relations are fading this is an issue that concerns you
our last encounter was but a little affair
we were shining as we stumbled from the bar
it was a lost cause without a final attempt

do you see that I cannot be on my own?
I fear the loneliness that builds inside
I feel torn apart and strung along
with every breathe I can find

when facing the problem, I say forgive me one last time
our last encounter was but a little affair
I keep calling just to see where you are
it was a lost cause without a final attempt
an attempt to be free

do you see that I cannot be on my own?
the loneliness that builds inside
I feel torn apart and strung along
with every breathe I can find

wanting, wishing, for one more
one more chance to set the record straight yet again
we're sinking, then swimming, it's a downward spiral
it was a lost cause without the final attempt
now were free

do you see that I cannot be on my own?
I fear the loneliness that builds inside
I feel torn apart and strung along
with every breathe I can find

DECIBAL DESIGN

creating is a gift for the arts of thought
a relationship that sticks is the hardest part
to make complete of a troubled spot
unchained melody, a glory daze

this song is about
our trials to break into
the common man's heart
to differentiate what
the contents about
the decibel design

the trials that break through
the tests of time
human culture
with reason and rhyme
taking a step off
the well-traveled path
a forgotten notion
freedom to reign

this song is about
our trials to break into
the common man's heart
to differentiate what
the contents about
the decibel design

searching the soul
belief in someone
to make you whole
no additional nights absurd
to be capable
and under control
freedom to reign

this song is about
our trials to break into
the common man's heart
to differentiate what
the contents about
the decibel design

LADDER

I can see straight up
when you're looking back on me
your vacant smile displays a verdict of guilty
you were too scared to be yourself
over analyzing what could be
I can't believe six months in
you'd go running out so rapidly
all the moments categorized as hard
wrapped up tightly in each other's arms
was it too much to take in?
you couldn't keep up your guard
see yourself through another's eyes
when you hold my hand
you hold on to
memories shared
from two different points of view
can you comprehend
I loved you
a girl brought up with fear and insecurity
does not know exactly what she wants
no goals she wants to achieve
besides having a bag of tricks up the sleeve
there is an excess of mind control
sliding razors across her wrists
that's all it took
we were side by side
after just one look

a newfound love to clasp onto
emotions were flying everywhere
we really cared
for the people we were
trying to be
see yourself through another's eyes
when you hold my hand
you hold on to
memories shared
from two different points of view
can you comprehend
I loved you

THE CHANGE

It seems in life there is always change
what once seemed so important
just doesn't feel the same
the people I knew when I was young
searched like fools trying to belong
momma raised me to be a good man
she said son one day you will understand

this morning's view
turns old into new
the restoration of youth
if I really didn't care
I wouldn't have been there
energy and attitude

the summer nights just seem to fade away
a hot July 4th on the coast of the lake
a crescent shaped moon cast over sandy shore
who could ask for anything more?
the soft embrace of Abigail's skin
lying next to mine

this morning's view
turns old into new
the restoration of youth
if I really didn't care
I wouldn't have been there
energy and attitude

THE PRICE IS RIGHT

price before value
come clean for a society view
scenes you don't believe
you soon become immune
there is the suffering too
as the substance runs through veins
denial of unconscious cravings

soon you can't escape
the body starts to shake
when all you can do is take
there is nothing left to give

I have learned by watching you
tell what I am supposed to do
the scenes I don't believe
the pain you seek and the
suffering the family goes through

soon you can't escape
the body starts to shake
when all you can do is take
there is nothing left to give

it's a little-known affliction
it just sucks you in
over time it turns into addiction

your underweight pale white skin
I can quit whenever I want to
I just need some time
that was the last thing he said
before he died

FALLING FOR YESTERDAY

I can still remember what it felt like
when you were cuddling into my side
the advantages and costs to
what might seem so simple and justified
sepia frames of you remain in pictures
frozen and untouched by hands of time
the years have passed and yet I keep finding myself
falling for yesterday

the seconds take the hours away
just fractions in a craze
well make amends somewhere
along the line I'd say

dreary afternoons filled with gray wash sky
her whispers in my ear and hair in my eye
I look for the sun to highlight her face
as tar fills my lungs, I miss that place

the seconds take the hours away
just fractions in a craze
well make amends somewhere
along the line I'd say

fall afternoons with overcast skies
crowded our vision and left us high and dry

my favorite stories were in the months of autumn
the season to change our lives forever more
now I look up to the sun to try to see her face
as tar fills my lungs, I miss that place

CHERITA

DEMO

2003

ASLEEP IN PEACE

If I only knew this would turn out
if I only knew that you wouldn't turn your back on me

when you just run away
from everyone that you've ever loved
I hope you sleep in peace
your point of living is living for yourself
yourself

cut the ribbon and our future starts
I set aside any regrets from my past
then I came to you cleansed and true
but you

run away
from everyone that you've ever loved
I hope you sleep in peace
your point of living is living for yourself
yourself

you tore down my walls and put faith in me
then you ripped out my heart
while I stuck by your side
and now I can't forgive
my best efforts retired
run away from all of those who care
I still can't believe after all of this

That I am still missing you standing there
Run

when you just run away
from everyone that you've ever loved
I hope you sleep in peace
your point of living is living for yourself
yourself

UNWIND

In passing these streets the lights swarm by
sad and lonely the child survives
he doesn't believe in sharing his thoughts
he's not quick to speak or be distraught
when he comes up to me with this look in his face
he says dad I can't seem to alleviate this pain

well my secret is to unwind
leave your thoughts far behind
because struggle surrounds the weak
we need to keep our focus

to understand is to comply
we have options we can't deny
each day is a gift we must receive
smile honest in disbelief
no reason for war all the time
to tell the truth or to tell a lie

well my secret is to unwind
leave your thoughts far behind
because struggle surrounds the weak
we need to keep our focus

to keep yourself
look into the limelight
I feel impaled

to focus on the silence
the silence
the silence surrounds the weak

well my secret is to unwind
leave your thoughts far behind
because struggle surrounds the weak
we need to keep our focus

COLORS IN THE SAND

the cloud covered skies
meet the cracks in the street
I'm consumed by what's being fed to me
through whispers in the wind
I'm dazed by pictures painted in front of me
these colors in the sand

sight to sound
my senses are intensified
miles from here
is where well find ourselves

spoken words utter last goodbyes
salt from the tears flowing down my face
it's here where I find my inner peace
its here where I'm incomplete

sight to sound
my senses are intensified
miles from here
is where well find ourselves

where well find ourselves
through sight or sound
well find a way
well find a way
well find away

from here
sight to sound
my senses are intensified
miles from here
is where well find ourselves

DANNY AND JUDDER

THE ORLANDO ALE

2002

Danny L. Judder L.

OPEN FLAME

So, you got a little taste of fame
how easily it can be taken away
when you're facing the open flame
burning the bridges your friends follow
down a hole
down an unholy hole
drift away
drift in haste
taken by flame

I don't know what's expected from
buying in till you can't have enough
speak to me I'm right here in front of you
just tell me what's on your mind
take your time

I am so tired of this superficial mix
I'll take myself out of the whirl
spotlights and whirlwinds
trying to have it all gets in the way
of a simple life with simple mistakes
the chaos is a driving force
pushing honesty away

I don't know what's expected from
buying in till you can't have enough
speak to me I'm right here in front of you

just tell me what's on your mind
take your time

I am so tired of this superficial mix
I'll take myself out of the whirl
spotlights and whirlwinds

TWO FACE ANOTHER

lying awake to see if this real
when I focus on the pain
to see if I still feel
I lay in bed for hours
do you remember
what you dream
I wanted to be someone
I wanted to be something i am not
I've wished for
I've searched for
I'm lost beside myself
well it seems so far away
when you're tired of being empty
I stretch, move around
I cant bring myself to my knees
I'm cold, I'm sore
I want something else
I can't have everything
I've wished for
I've searched for
I'm lost beside myself
well it seems so far away
when you're tired of being empty
before this over
please wait for
I'm starting all over
please erase my mind

I don't know why this is
I don't know
I shouldn't care
if I could only
wake myself up today
wake myself up
two face another day
two face another day

DOUGHNUTS/DONUTS

Doughnuts are good
doughnuts are good
in the morning
in the evening
doughnuts are great
doughnuts are great
when you a masturbating
doughnuts are good
when your reading a newspaper
doughnuts are phenomenal
when you are sitting on the pot waiting for the mail
I'm waiting for the mail
waiting for the mail
I'm waiting for the mail
so, I'll eat a doughnut
it may be a Krispy Kreme or even a dunkin donut
donuts well eat em well
they are good with milk and coffee
Judder sing the song
Judder sing it soft
this one
Judder don't sing it wrong
so, Judder sing the song
about doughnuts and the crème
about coffee and the cigarettes
the spoken words between
a coffee shop nearby home from walking distance we both know

and still I cannot have my last vent
a dollar short what time is spent
and in this time
we can cement the bond that's formed
I don't think I can explain to you what this means to me
a coffee we must share
a spoken word between
you've got my doughnut you'd better give it back man
cigarettes and crème
I'm pretty pissed off I paid a dollar fifty for this refill
I'm going to eat another doughnut
Even when the po-po walks in the door
I'm going to eat my donut
even though he wants it
he can't have my donut
because it is mine
the spoken words between
donuts and coffee
things that go without saying
I can't help but say I'm sorry
I'm sorry
Doughnuts are my thing
I keep them in my house
I'm shelving the donuts
Bigger than a mouse
Krispy Kreme I slash my wrists
I wake up for that shit in the morning
ducking the donuts
Krispy crème coffee and a cigarette
coffee and cigarettes
while reading a newspaper
a new trap for that mouse that is bigger than my donut

8625 SUMMERWALK

Were in a new place now
Everything seems different somehow
Passing cars in the streets
We are standing still
Life in a different space
Surrounded by unfamiliar faces
We are screaming silently
Pleading for happy while anguished
My soul fades away
I have nothing more to say
I have been waiting her for you to call me

CAREER DAY

These paths are chosen
but are bonds remain unbroken
because my friends we are for certain
that are jobs are a burden

Lead or follow
and so, we leave the rest behind
and say so long to the times
well remain unbroken

I am hearing voices
persuading my choices
they ask what's sounds good to me
and I never know
who I will grow up to be?
my stars will show
should I

Lead or follow
and so we leave the rest behind
and say so long to the times
well remain unbroken

Lead, Lead, Lead
Lead or follow
Lead or follow
Lead or follow

STILL FRAMES

I wish you would lay and be still
were sold and we cannot turn back right now
from

wealth or pride
still frames of you
walk or drive
still frames of you
is it worth the time?
these still frames of you are blind

when starved for attention
well stage a feud
then the still frames of emptiness
will correlate with truth

wealth or pride
still frames of you
walk or drive
still frames of you
is it worth the time?
these still frames of you are blind
your blind
you lie
for

wealth or pride
still frames of you
walk or drive
still frames of you
is it worth the time?
these still frames of you aren't blind

your blind
you lie
fool

THE WORLD IS
STANDING STILL

Sometimes
it feels as though the world has left me here
I'm standing still
please stay for awhile
tell me the other stories side
what is so shameful
is how grateful I am that its gone
why am I so tired?
what day is this again
adhesive is so hard to break
hey jealousy makes the difference

let your world just fall apart
into the wreckage of the heart
disarmed by what has been misled
a servant or a saint

your home
your heart
your high

let your world just fall apart
into the wreckage of the heart
disarmed by what has been misled
a servant or a saint

THE BALLAD OF SUMMERWALK

we find ourselves awake
unforeseen by the darkness cast
when I focus on the pain
to see if I am real
do you remember I couldn't sleep?
I wanted to be someone
I wanted to be something I am not

I wished for
I've searched for
I'm lost looking for myself
now it seems so far away
tired of being empty

I've switched from lying down
I can't bring myself to my knees
I'm cold, I'm sore
I want something else
I can't have everything
before this over
could you please wait
this could be over
so please wait
I'm starting it over
please don't waste my time

I don't know why it is so important
to wake myself up today
wake myself up again and face another day

I wished for
I've searched for
I'm lost looking for myself
now it seems so far away
tired of being empty
tired of being empty

THE BALLAD OF SUMMERWALK PT. 2

Lying awake
to see if I am still here
I focus on the pain to see if still feel
oh my
then I remember why I could not sleep
I wanted to be something
I wanted to be something more than me
I wished for and I have searched for
I am still looking for myself
but it seems so far to me
that I am tired of being empty
I sit lying down
I cannot bring myself to my knees
I am cold I'm sore
I want something else
I cannot have anything
please wait lord
please help me
before this over
please pray for me
this could be over
please waste my time
I do not know why this is
I don't know and I don't care
if I could only

wake myself up today
wake myself up
wake myself up to
face another day
to face another day

DANNYS SONG

We're riding off in a storm
through millions of faces
of people I've seen before
I'm casually forgetting to remember one more
reason for the notion that I'm feeling so sore
it all amounts to nothing but subsequently it is something
mystery in ice sculptures
the rain is like an ocean crashing to the ground
following the footsteps of everyone walking to doors
I'm talking to myself like I have never spoken before
I'm casually forgetting to remember one more
reason for the notion that I'm feeling so sore
it all amounts to nothing but subsequently it is something

WOODCHUCK

I need a drink
Drink you better take a drink you woodchuck
Woodchuck could chuck Wood chuck wood I eat wood
I like wood motherfucker
Wood chuck wood chuck I like wood
I like wood motherfucker
Woodchuck could chuck Wood chuck could chuck wood
Hey motherfucker you
You like wood well so do I
Hahaha what is that
its wood
wood is good wood is great
when you're sitting around with great of people
and they like to eat wood
wood? what is that smell
eh its wood
its wood I like wood how about you
I like wood we all do too
wood its wood
this is where the story turns around
this is where the story turns around
turns around turns around turns around
this is where the story turns around turns around
I don't why it doesn't turn around turns around
this is where the story turns around and everybody get sad
and they cry and they miss their parents
and they miss playing with elephants playing with elephants

and washing their nuts with sponges
eating broccoli with forks and cheese
and cheese and cheese and butter
oh, smoked sausages in the microwave
I got smoked sausages in the microwave
in the microwave
Before the crave of hunger
Mmm In the unger
underneath my pillow
I keep toothpicks and sandpaper cheese
and cheese and cheese
because I love mozzarella
and quesadillas with my cheese and sour cream
at night a craving in my kitchen it calls out to me
I crave the hunger beneath my hair it makes so fucking
I'm hungry I'm hungry I'm hungry I'm hungry I'm hungry
no shit I could go for fucking a bacon cheeseburger and some mashed
potatoes
broccoli and cheese and potatoes and peas
and cheese and peas and cheese and peas
I like to eat peas and sometime when I pet the dog, I get fleas
oh, my got it really sucks I can't believe it happened
cheeseburger macaroni apple juice and sausage ha-ha
dude you think your funny
no, I don't
yeah you do
what
yes man
look at your fucking face
fuck you man
hey man you're not fucking cool
you think your all that but your nothing but a piece of shit
piece of stool piece of stool
he's not a piece of shit
he's a piece of stool piece of stool
piece of stool piece of stool

he's not a piece of shit
he's a piece of stool piece of stool
isn't that cool isn't that cool
I don't care
look under your shoe and you're going to see what is left
I'm going to take your head and wrap it around
you're going to make me so mad that I'm going to hit you in the head
with a big fucking baseball bat
come go on and test me I'm going to take you to my level
I'm going to hit you in the head with my big ole shovel
that is right you messed with the wrong guy
I'm not going to take any more of this fucking shit from you now
you stepped to wrong guy and I'm going to kick you in the nuts
nuts nuts
kick you in the fucking nuts

MY LAST BEER

hey man you took my last beer
yeah man I'm sorry I didn't mean to
you're a bastard
it was so tempting it was all cold and frosty and I'm really thirsty
but that was my last beer
dude I'm sorry man I'll get you another one when I turn 21
man you're not going to be 21 for like 3 months at least
I know man but ill get you 2 beers
that's not the point
I just took his last beer
took it right out of the fridge
you just took my last beer
I'm sorry man
You'd better be fucking sorry because you're a prick
Well I can't help it sometimes I stoop low
sometimes I take other peoples belongings
yeah you do you better not do that again anymore or I'll have to kick
you in the nuts man
don't kick me in the nuts I'm sorry I took your last beer la la la la
is there a skip in the song here we go
Heineken do equis are not domestic beers
something and something and something la la la la la
cuz this is drunken beer song I obviously took the last one
I was already fucked up
Anheuser busch bud light do you like coors light and domestic
beer import do you like imports I don't know what I am saying amstel
light beers

190

he doesn't know what he's saying what's he's saying
really he's sorry he took that last beer
what he's saying nobody knows
what he's saying nobody's knows
nobody what he is saying
what he is saying
what he's saying nobody's knows
what he is saying
what he is saying, and nobody knew why he took that last beer
nobody knows

TO REGAIN MY VISION

I am falling back on these hopes
and all these fears of that someone
the stole my heart & broke me down
and I will take them back I will somehow
I face my fears one day at a time
they appear and broke me down
what gives what takes over your heart
I do not know what it is that makes it so hard
to break hard to face once again you are in sin
why is this haunting me
why is this haunting me and holding me back from within
I will take this challenge and face my fears upfront
the funk in contagious my whole world is shame
and my dreams are what is taken from this mindless soul
disregard what I am saying
my life as I live take one step at a time

4FIT

EMOTIONAL DISPLAY
OF SOUND

2002

Danny L. Kelly S.
Shane M. Judder L.

CREATE SOUND

If you're not building your ambitions up
then you are probably breaking down to size
what it is and what it always was
you should not get caught up in the times that have passed
why not try to sit back, relax your cares
I don't know why wont
why don't you try

I feel
I fear
that what's at stake is something you could make
create sound
what's in store is what we can't ignore
create sound
our sound

If you're not building your ambitions up
then you are probably breaking down to size
what it is and what it never was
do not get caught up in the times that have passed
why not try to sit back, relax, and just don't care
I don't know why wont
why don't you try

I feel
I fear
that what's at stake is something you could make

create sound
what's in store is what we can't ignore
create sound
our sound

look into my eyes and tell me what you see
is everything really ok
rip your eyes because this kid you cannot see
not everything is ok

ARE WE THERE

I never sought what was promised to me
because it's too late to turn back into the cold
we often contradict living conditions for ourselves
but you know I'm too scared that I might be growing old

are we there?
are we there?
are we there?

who thought this could end?
who thought we would fall?
who thought at all?
who thought this could end?
who thought we would fall?
our interest in song

It's the same when you look back upon your life
another year is washed aside
who's to blame
when you look back upon this life
and there was no one standing beside you

are we there?
are we there?
are we there?
now

who thought this could end?
who thought we would fall?
who thought at all?
who thought this could end?
who thought we would fall?
our interest in song
on and on and on

THIS PERFECT

see lights embedding
come closer into the shade of better things yet to come
well dreams are scattered out and streaming thin
upon memories scarce and few again
unsure why things are always messed up and broken about
unsure why things are always messed up

Blue seas are pristines of beauty
when everything is all fucked up
Blue seas are pristines of beauty
when everything is all fucked up

living in this perfect world and standing in the rain
my tears are hidden in this thunderstorm
well I'll wait for clear skies and golden suns
when I should be really
unsure why things are always messed up and broken about
unsure that I've never seen such beauty!

Blue seas are pristines of beauty
when everything is all fucked up
Blue seas are pristines of beauty
when everything is all fucked up

everything is all fucked up
everything is all fucked up
everything is all fucked up

everything that's true
everything is all fucked up
everything is all fucked up
everything is all fucked up
everything you know
I'm not really here
Blue seas are prestines of beauty
when everything is all fucked up
Blue seas oh
everything is all fucked up
everything is all fucked up
everything is all fucked up
everything that's true
everything is all fucked up
everything is all fucked up
everything is all fucked up
everything you know
I'm not really here

T.R.O.N.

He wrote to many words
about his guilt
I sold my soul
so, we can grow
what we reap and sow
through many stars
we challenge what is real
is it coincidence or fate?

we all fall to our knees
it light of dreams we pray daily
a bastard son is me
despite the scenes we cannot change

I was a little boy
until my father's blood was spilled
we shall not steal
we shall not kill
the trucks wreckage revealed
that

we all fall to our knees
it light of dreams we pray daily
a bastard son is me
despite the scenes we cannot change

I should have let forever know
he could not stay forever though
I should have let forever know
he could not let forever go

EMERSON THEATER

It is sad your leaving
it's open season
every time I think
I am going psycho
I'm crazy or is that what you think

Still I search to find but it seems there is no hope
Not everything is ok
But you do not know what it's like
to sink deep inside
This empty carcass with a struggling soul
It eats me away

So far, I realize that everything is a waste
Still sore I realize that everything is not ok

Sore it feels
Sore I feel
Sore it tastes

It's sad your leaving
it's open season
every time I think
Am I going psycho?
Am I crazy or is that what you think?

So far, I realize that everything is a waste
Still sore I realize everything is not ok

4FIT

DEPARTURE FROM NORMALITY

2001

Danny L. Kelly S. Shane M. Judder L.

DARKEST SCARS

their haunting and feeding
famine spoils the healing
wait release the peace or cease at least
the gift of birth question what's its worth
cause I'm fucked up in the head
a manic depressant I see no positive and if I do, I regret it
and this is why I will cry
that's right because

I tried to win but I lost
I tried to save myself the cost
in living life in total fear
my darkest scars they reappear
reappear

you see inside me
wanting just sleeping
all day long its easy
wait release the peace or cease at least
the gift of birth question what its worth
with this diseased mind I'm broken up
a cynic approach to whatever comes up
one more try I'll do it again but we all know
that's right because

I tried to win but I lost
I tried to save myself the cost

in living life in total fear
my darkest scars they reappear
reappear

you see inside me
you see inside me
you see inside me
I am sad and I feel so alone
reaching in the darkest part
I'm living this the darkest art
of a body filled with grayish skin
a pray to god my life will end
no! no!
fall down can't inspire this desire fall
that's right because

I tried to win but I lost
I tried to save myself the cost
in living life in total fear
my darkest scars they reappear
reappear you see inside me

STARLIGHT

Everyday it's the same old story you feel guilty, a bit nervous.
Everyday it's the same old thinking
that there is no point this
but my starlight!

It doesn't make much sense, much sense!
Always asking why?
always looking for something, something!
when you should just

See the way things are then look up to the stars
See the way things are then look up to the stars
look to the stars
look to the stars
the stars
just
see the way things are the look up to the stars
see the way things are the look up to the stars
look to the stars
look to the stars

I am sick, of my self-pity, taking hold, and clinging to me.
Don't give up and be strong, just let it out, when it comes along.
Reach in yourself and find the light that will shine for days even
when it's not bright.

All you need!
Is right above!
shining into you!
when times are tough!

see the way things are then look up to the stars
see the way things are then look up to the stars
see the way things are then look up to the stars
see the way things are then look up to the stars
look up to the
look up to the stars, stars

DEPARTURE FROM NORMALITY

I lost my self again
I lost my self again
I lost my self again
I lost my self again
and the door swings open to things inside
I'm tripled up and broken down for all to see
for all to see
in a mix matched dark room it's hard to reconcile
all these expectations, I'm disappointed all the time

Live for us while I cant
look to find myself
live for us still I can't look to find

just rely on uncertainty, I'm scared sometimes
departure from normality, salient and supplied
don't try to run away, away from the hidden guides
the guides surprise adversive smiles

Live for us while I can't
look to find myself
live for us still I can't look to find
the selfish choices are the last ones made
in the final decision I regret I didn't stay
regret I did not stay

as I lay here wondering when will the answers come
well you ask the wrong questions? you shouldn't worry so much
Live for us while I can't
look to find myself
live for us still I can't look to find

just rely on uncertainty, I'm scared sometimes
departure from normality, salient and supplied
uncertainty for sure I'm scared that I can't control
uncertainty for sure I'm scared that I can't control
uncertainty for sure I'm scared that I can't control
uncertainty for sure I'm scared that I can't control
control I can't control!

Live for us while I can't
look to find myself
live for us still I can't look to find

look into his eyes
look into her eyes
then look into my eyes
and tell me what you see

DON'T SAY

well I said these words
just think about the things you've never heard
these last times with her
if I could think out loud, I'd say

say
what! what about what about
the things I should have said
what! what about what about
the things I don't
say don't say I could never

the last times we go
down to the past and all it holds
please open up myself
one more time before I'd say

say
what! what about what about
the things I should have said
what! what about what about
the things I don't
say don't say I could never

say
don't say
don't say

I could never
Say
don't say
don't say
I could never!
say
what! what about what about
the things I should have said
what! what about what about
the things I don't
say don't say I could never

say don't say don't say I could never
say don't say don't say I could never

SILHOUETTE

You don't know what it's like
to be living in poverty
this is the way I am
You don't know what it's like
to be living without a family
this is the way I live
Last six months haven't been
shit to me, so here's my philosophy
this is the way I am
My girlfriend just said goodbye
to me so please don't fucking lie to me
this is the way I live

Blame myself its always my fault
Can't live with this I've set myself up
Blame myself its always my fault
Can't live with this I've set myself up

You don't know my friends
and me we get so sad you see
this is the way I am
sometimes I get so pissed off
at me when you just can't talk to me
this is the way live
lost my home at age 19 so please
don't you comfort me
this is the way I am

so, if you wonder what's wrong
with me ask yourself what you would think
this is the way I live

Blame myself its always my fault
Can't live with this I've set myself up
Blame myself its always my fault
Can't live with this I've set myself up

I am your silhouette
I am your silhouette
I am your silhouette
I am your silhouette
You don't know what it's like
to be living in poverty
this is the way I am
You don't know what it's like
to be living without a family
this is the way I live
Last six months haven't been
shit to me, so here's my philosophy
this is the way I am
My girlfriend just said goodbye
to me so please don't fucking lie to me
this is the way I live

Blame myself its always my fault
Can't live with this I've set myself up
Blame myself its always my fault
Can't live with this I've set myself up

BETTER DAYS WILL COME

each day goes on once shared
not everything is ok
so please move on away
we will end in hate
I hate everything about me right now
for a while I've been here
without you I'll make it
we are not here to make it impossible
we are out here on our own
each day goes on displayed
some decisions made in stride we'll pray
you can't stop me now
from moving on insane
it's better this way we'll make it today forever

for a while I've been here
without you I'll make it
we're not here to make it impossible
we're not here to know
like me
leave me alone

for a while I've been here
without you I'll make it
we're not here to make it impossible
we're not here to know
like me

leave me alone
it may not be possible
it may not be possible
it may not be possible
it may not be possible
it may not be possible
it may not be possible
it may not be possible
that better days will come

LEFT TO SUFFER

it is safe to say you love her so
we plead ourselves off no remorse
in searching for this one true night
in leaving her you suffer alone

Fall
I care for her

the way it feels with you next to me
a certain sense of security
from two worlds this bond is formed
if you believe in me, you'll suffer apart

Fall to your knees
I care for her
Crawl back please
I'm left to suffer alone

You Fall to your knees
I care for her
Crawl back please
I'm left to suffer alone

MY CONDOLENCES

he's lost at home
no hope or tenderness
he yearns for a soft caress
he can't explain what is wrong
trembling from a different view
he's struggling through
but crumbling still

it's not his fault
his childhood was bad
these signals out cry

family shows no concern
lessons he can't unlearn
the vicious cycle taught to him
when all effort seems to fail
the gun prevails
these signals out cry

it's not his fault
his childhood was bad
these signals out cry

the media asked were their symptoms
no, how we portray our victims
no, the great war is the great depression
my god, please forgive him

GOODBYE

so, you were sitting there franticly stressing
and asking yourself why
it must always be goodbye
just say you are sorry it really cannot be that bad
we cannot take for granted all the good times
the sky is the limit in this here dramatic fight
the long road ahead is cluttered with stop signs
I've seen the effect cheer insults
you always talked trash about those who were needy
but strangely enough you needed more than most
attention, appreciation, acceptance, to boot
the only person I think you fooled was you

the teen runs but she can not
figure out what it is
she is running from
the teen runs but she can not
run

run, run, run
accept the failure
run, run, run,
was there anything
run, run, run,
was there anyone
that you didn't count out
run, run, run

stop, listen, this lack of love
you can't rise above the emptiness
you feel deep inside
but you need to realize what it is inside
that you need to look out for
you need to realize how act you to others
it's horrible
be the exception

the teen runs but she can not
figure out what it is
she is running from
the teen runs but she can not
run

4FIT

A STRUGGLE WITHIN

1999

Danny L. Kelly S.
Keith V. Judder L.

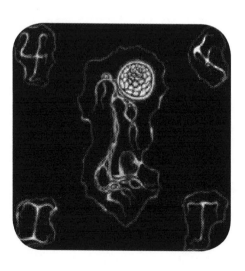

ANXIETY

I can feel this in me
intoxicated and not knowing why the
Hippocrates surround me
faded and losing obnoxious times I die
but anxiety intrigues me
this loss of control burning down on me
cause I can feel this in me
the knowledge to feel to want to RISE!

your lies burn eyes take mine (x4)

lost days hypnotize thieves
my accidents in white collar crime
forgotten facts divide minds
sympathy in social situations
upon city lines we
rise above here slowly
unexplained early deaths in delinquent days
but carpet bag my envy
on probation the juveniles will RISE!

your lies burn eyes take mine (x4)

I can feel this
things coming back down on me from
all the pressure
all the stress building up

I can't hold it in
I must release these things held up in this head
but last time I said it don't you forget it
I want to rise

your lies burn eyes take mine (x7)

RISE!

FX 45

the confusion has stuck
what the fuck I disregard these previous mood swings
Dream sequence I contemplate
cause I have no answers to questions I cause
Disconnect before you recollect
the function of the truth be misunderstood
you know sympathy and the thoughts that count
cannot connect me to what I have found.

I go back to the beat coming up off the street
Yall, we got the attitudes to keep it real
so, you envision the outside you kick it
and jump slide the indie he used was a meltdown
experience everything you need
kick it up off the curbs that bleed
nobody tells me shit
disillusion is next up
shut up I said to the fucker bitching at me
skated around there is nothing to do
cause I have no answers to questions i cause
life's unfair and its uncontrolled
so, deal with it
maybe if you can hold, I pray constantly nothing about
still cannot connect me to what I found

under the shift in Mellon collie skin
victims that step up get pushed down
again, nothing is wrong when nothing is right
hatred for a brother emptiness
inside the basic needs that I've never known
the roots to this seed could never be grown
adrenaline rises when confidence falls
do not debate this with me
I have lost the draw
never knowing what is in store
who could ask for something more?
sectioned off
unstable and thrown away

go back to the beat you-all
we got the attitudes to keep it real
so, you envision the outside
you kick it and jump slide
the indie he used was a meltdown
experience all the things you need

or keep to yourself indeed
nobody tells me shit
so, it
it was the last straw

back to the beat coming up off the street
yes, back to the beat coming off your street
yes, back to the beat coming up off the street
next up
and 45

SOCIOPATH

staring back onto you
you're the best thing I've ever known
I give you all that I can
but it doesn't mean a thing so long
all your faces displace the past I want to know
I'd give it another chance but
two chances mean nothing your gone

I gave it all to you (x3)
it's all for you

looking back on the times we've shared in another place
I'm feeling so empty I cannot begin to express create
empty thoughts and unspoken words this is all I know
so, what should I do to help this feeling go die?

I gave it all to you (x3)
it's all for you

everything was lie,
and everything was lie,
and everything you've said and
done for me, because everything was I lie
now I want to know

you! it's all for you (x4)

I'm the only one

FISTED

fisted motherfucker must resist his fist or
to disgrace the race, he said
he wanted to bruise my face
showing off the pride of an unconscious soul
never knowing the senses that he should go
step up and loss of reality
in his sanity a lost cause
the clues and the final straws

belief in the thief
to succeed in a society of greedy need
you say, you said
from all of you that hurt in pain
fuck all of you unite today
from all of you that hurt in pain
fuck all of you your fists away

fisted motherfucker must resist his fist or
to disgrace the race, he said
he wanted to bruise my face
showing off the pride of an unconscious soul
never knowing the senses that he should go
step up and loss of reality
in his sanity a lost cause
the clues and the final straws

belief in the thief
to succeed in a society of greedy need
you say, you said
from all of you that hurt in pain
fuck all of you unite today
from all of you that hurt in pain
fuck all of you your fists away

all of you, hurt in pain
all of you, unite today
all of you hurt in pain
all of you, your fists away
put your fists away
you say, you said

from all of you that hurt in pain
fuck all of you unite today
from all of you that hurt in pain
fuck all of you your fists away

let it go man, let it go man
don't want to bring up to the next level
let it go man, let it go man
don't want to see me slip and put a fist in him
let it go man, let it go man
don't want to bring up to the next level
let it go man, let it go man
don't want to see me slip and put a fist in him

FED UP WITH YOU

a perfect gift guilt view
I seize it first receive too few
unjust this is why
I hate to try
but pay for it
you've come this far

fed up with you
I get pushed on the floor
fed up with you
come on ask me some more
fed up with you
I'm confined in this
fed up with you
I deserve more

a burden slaps my hand
I talk to myself
I wish for quick death
renew cut himself
the mandate court
wish for more but it's all been said

fed up with you
I get pushed on the floor
fed up with you
come on ask me some more

fed up with you
I'm confined in this
fed up with you
I deserve more shit

don't give in (x11)

right
I'm falling, I'm falling
right
I'm falling, I'm falling
right
I'm falling, I'm falling
right
right out of view

VHISTLER

4Fit coming straight from the underground
we've got to step it up with a new sound
lyrics are the trick to keep the hits and some schizo hit
because were 4 kids doing are best
compete with rest motherfuckers detest
all the followers infest my mind my soul my heart
and so, we try to complete this independence apart

2,3,4, 4Fit coming straight from the underground
we've got to step it up with a new sound
issues of concern you earn learn
or you will burn up and down
get up and down up and down and side to side
despise those visions of your eyes
what does it take to rise above?
my faith in friends and their honest love
stop

4Fit is the last chance about
you'll were coming for real and not selling out
we're bringing the noise and the hottest beats
step up motherfuckers or face defeat
we've been pushed down for way to long
I hate this view of all that's wrong
but were 4Fit and we will rise above
with our faith in fans and their honest love
vhistler

IN CONCLUSION

I cannot take this because it's holding me back
to the last days that I had being with him
and I try to avoid the constant strain in me
from missing you and wishing you were with me
Mourn this loss
cause I take this all alone
Mourn this loss
cause I can't fight these feelings on my own
on my own

I cannot forget the times you've held me tight
securing me from the black crazed stormy nights
keeping me safe and pointing the way to promised
life of care and devotion

Mourn this loss
cause I take this all alone
Mourn this loss
cause I can't fight these feelings on my own
on my own
why did I grow up living this way?
I ask myself that every single day
and when I think of you hope is all
I have that you were proud of the
youngest son you had
Go! I cannot control the hate I have
for the methods life uses and abuses
all the things I had they fell apart
depart gone in a single
I'm pissed off that the world revolves this way
because kills my heart and it smashes my esteem
I was deprived,
deprives of a part of me
but I'm trying to do what's right
I'm giving my best not to ignite
and blame the others for my confusion in
mourning times there is no solution
conclusion
and I can't take this
it's unfair
I'm always fighting for this
life's despair in you, you

FARMERS SONG

All Right
I Went Down To The Farm To Get Myself A Chicken
I Wopped His Head Right Off And It Was Finger Lickin Good And
It Was Good
And The Chicken Says Bock Bock Ba Gock
Bock Bock Ba Gock Bock Bock Ba Gock
Bock Bock Ba Gock
Bock Bock Bock Bock Bock
I Went Down To The Farm To Get Myself Some Bacon
I Found The Farmers Wife And Said
Damn Bitch What You Makin
Ooh Bacon And It Was Good
And The Piggy Says Oink Oink And Squeel
Oink Oink And Squeel
Oink Oink And Squeel
Oink Oink And Sqeel
Oink Oink Oink Oink Oink
Ooh And It Was Good
I Went Down To The Farm To Get Myself Some Beef
I Got Myself A Steer And I Grabbed Him By The Teeth
And He Was Good To
And The Cow Says Moo Moo Moo Moo
Moo Moo Moo Moo
Moo Moo Moo Moo
Moo Moo Moo Moo
And It Was Good

SEDIMENT

Self Titled

1998

Ben N. Dusty S. Ryan N. Matt K. Judder L.

NOBODY CARES

Does anybody care that I don't care anymore my mind wonders
aimlessly as I stare at the floor right now, I want to be somewhere else?
somewhere else?
does anybody care that I don't care anymore my mind wonders
aimlessly as I stare at the floor right now, I want to be somewhere else?
somewhere else
in the garage or in my basement where I can play, and no one cares
I want to be like johnny d
I want to be like Billy joe
I want to be in the front row
in the front row of all our shows
I want to be on magazines
I want to know what being a star means
I want to see myself on MTV
I want to move to the west coast
where are sorrows turn into ghosts
a place where no one cares what I do
we could be the Deftones
we could like Weezer to
we could be anything just not for you
I want to move to Bremerton and get a record deal
play all the clubs we can find
ill bleach my hair and get some tattoos
do whatever the fuck I want to do go
I want to be like johnny d
I want to be like Billy joe
I want to be in the front row

in the front row of all our shows
I want to be on magazines
I want to know what being a star means
I want to see myself on MTV
fuck MTV

CONTAGIOUS

Don't 2 wrongs make a right
then why do we have to fight
I realize what I did was wrong
now I have to write you a fucking song
before you slap me you should know
that next time I'll take it slow
so, don't you worry about us
because our love is contagious
If 2 wrongs make a right, then why do we have to fight
and maybe what I did was wrong so I now I have to write you this song
but why do things end up like this
because our love is dangerously contagious
when you and I meet next time
whether it be for rain or shine
we will look into each other's eyes
we will never want to say goodbye
then you'll slap me and I'm okay
because I'll just look the other way
I'll ask you what the hell is wrong
then I'll write you another song
If 2 wrongs make a right, then I realize we have to fight
and maybe what I did was wrong so I now I have to write you this song
but why do things end up like this because our love is dangerously
contagious
If 2 wrongs make a right, then I realize we have to fight
and maybe what I did was wrong so I now I have to write you this song
but why do things end up like this because our love is dangerously
contagious

KATIE

I heard you don't like boys
tell me is this true
I saw you wearing a pink triangle
and to think I used to like you
you have probably never heard of MXPX
you have probably never heard of BLINK 182
and to think I used to like you
and I said Katie what made you think this way
Katie why can't you be straight for just one day
I heard you have a girlfriend now
I heard you have sex with her somehow
I wonder if you are ever going to change
or do lesbians just stay the same
I said Katie what made you think this way
Katie why you cannot be straight for just one day
Oh, OH No
You had such a pretty face
but you let it go to waste
It's too bad you're a lesbian at heart
because I liked you from the very start
you are the only girl I've ever loved
the only girl I ever dream of
but you had to go ruin it all
Katie you are my downfall
I said Katie what made you think this way
Katie why cannot you be straight for just one day
Oh, Oh NO

244

JUNCTION 231

There they sit at the junction seeking for some satisfaction
she leans back and lets out a sigh he hears the silence and wonders why
out from a box emerges a smoke he's lived his life with the common
folk
the dead quiet time just seems to drag on
what they once had now appears to be gone
it's a shame that I can't sleep and your to blame
what now is slightly grey
your turn its ok back now at the start
we once close but now apart
the old days and memories
their no more fuck the speech
take this gift and hold them tight
to your dismay I won the fight
it all seemed like a vivid dream
not everything is what is it seems
There they sit at the junction seeking for some satisfaction
she leans back and lets out a sigh he hears the silence and wonders why
out from a box emerges a smoke he's lived his life with the common
folk
the dead quiet time just seems to drag on
what they now had now appears to be gone
smoothed out and now its fine
now gone what was mine
turned up inside out
smack down right in front
so long it was great

too bad likely fate
it was dark now its dawn
It what was here now is gone
take this gift and hold them tight
to your dismay I won the fight
it all seemed like a vivid dream
not everything is what is it seems

PERSONAL HELL

can someone help me
come get me out
help me soon before I have to shout
locked in this room from 8 to 3
this place is ruled by tyranny
I hate the ruler
I hate the chief
I hate the servants kissing his feet
I don't wanna be a troublemaker
I have my point of view and you won't take her
just let me life my life the way way I want to
and I promise I won't grow up like you
mom and dad
why won't you let me out
do you like to hear me scream and shout?
what did I do to make you this mad?
as a kid was I really that bad
you say you love me
it is for the best
but I don't wanna turn up like the rest
I don't wanna be a troublemaker
I have my point of view and you won't take her
just let me life my life the way way I want to
and I promise I won't grow up like you
let's go
so now the guards they think I'm crazy
I try to tell them I'm just lazy

Some of the inmates make fun of me
But I guess that is the way it has to be
I don't care what others think
They suggest I see a shrink
I'm still trapped up inside this jail cell
And now I live in my own personal hell

NEGATIVE CREEP

Feelings hid deep inside of me
because of all that bullshit you perceive
I see this town each and every day
Not got one positive thing to say
Now you've got me wrapped around your finger
what will you do with me now?
Unleash a strange hold from hell
release me from this shit town cell
they think were losers and they think we suck
they might be right, but we don't give a fuck we try to be trendy
we try to fit in they laugh at us and we drink again
we call it home and it's all we got
burn this down with just one shot
drown our troubles away again and again
it gets kind of old but in the end
it's what we come back for as long as we get fucked up and torn
they think were losers and they think we suck
they might be right, but we don't give a fuck we try to be trendy
we try to fit in they laugh at us and we drink again
they all make fun of us
because we play on Friday night
but there is nothing else to do
because this town dies at midnight
I just need some time away
from being locked up every day
I could never forget my whiskey shot
its sometimes the only friend that I've got

what have you done for me?
this town is so damn boring
they think were losers and they think we suck
they might be right, but we don't give a fuck we try to be trendy
we try to fit in they laugh at us and we drink again

BACK

turned around and saw my fate
it was there and I took the bait
lost my way so here I sit
I had it there and I can't get back!
it threw me for such a loop, but I can't believe I lost it in just one night
but anyway, its stuck like this intense dream should I just go back to the
place I started well I think not
it blows right past and then I turn around (x3)
past its time for me to move right on
I've had my fun back in the day so far away
unfortunate it feels like the wind here in my face
I can't lose the dream that I'd like to erase
oh, such a shame
spit please can you come help me get rid of the thoughts that stick in my head
I really need your help in this time of need
can you get some pills to calm this craze?
I thank you much bitch
I turned back around and saw my fate
it was there so I took the bait
lost my way and here I sit
when I had it there and I can't get back!
I could turn right back but that wouldn't
solve anything anyway well I know now
the clear path that I should take
so nice to find the best way to go to get back

251

spit please can you come help me get rid of the thoughts that stick in my head
I really need your help in this time of need
can you get some pills to calm this craze?
please help me
can you please
please help me
can you please
please help me
can you please
please help me
can you please
help me get back
that's right back off into it
back when I get back
I get backed off
backed off and beat in the middle
I get backed off and beat in the middle
I get backed off and beat in the middle
I get back off!

A POINTLESS LIFE
ANOTHER FRIEND

He thought he loved that damn girl so much
but now he realized he was wrong
She is so dearly departed
in an instant she had to go and steal
my heart
now go and leave me alone
By myself is the way to be
I can't count on anyone but me
A pointless another's friend
Getting caught up in the confusion
life is hard it takes getting used to
A pointless life another's friend
So now go down that lonely road
It's certainly a means to an end
And I have lost my friend
By myself is the way to be
I can't count on anyone but me
A pointless another's friend
Getting caught up in the confusion
life is hard it takes getting used to
A pointless life another's friend

JUDDER ML

RANDOM MIND CAPTURED SCRIBBLES AND JOURNALING LETTERS AND CARDS POST ITS AND NAPKINS

1992-2005

ZERO

On this day Jan 22. I feel as if someone has stabbed me with all the problems in the world. I went into a sudden rush of speed grabbed some old boxes and went through them all in a violent surge of happiness yet unfulfilled sadness. Then once I was done going down memory lane the happiness was over, and my present returned. Those thoughts made me loose it☹ The million memories swarmed through my head like a giant Cumulus cloud over the tropical rainforest. I had to slow down settle down and grab a pen and paper. I began writing this increasingly common effect of this world on me. As I scroll through dozens of little post it notes all I can say is this world sucks. I hate myself but I want to live. I hate everything around me and I make myself physically sick with new and amazing problems. The childlike wonder is gone, and I repeatedly ask why do I feel this way? I write sudden stupid words in my head down and hang them on the walls. The walls of this all mighty room that both cares, kills, and consumes me. Everything that I can find goes in my room and it holds my many memories. I store all my thoughts in this small wooden box. All these scribbles and words are making me weird as the substance soaks my bloodstream. I am slowly sedated to a calm, cool, normal, state of mind. I write these words because after this spell is over then there would be no other way to describe this phenomenon. The evidence of such an instance would be removed the exhale of my breath. This occasional event in anyway would be erased from existence. These are the words of this fool.

THE KILLER IN ME IS THE KILLER IN YOU

Now I am flipping out shaking and losing my mind
I can only listen to the same old some on repeat to calm my nerves
I only want to cry and go away
Why, am I so down that I cannot write anymore
my mind is simply to distorted
my past, I want to be 14 again now maybe forever
I just cannot remain that age that pisses me off
off to the point of no return
just leave me alone
I cannot take it all
I cannot take any more of my body's crap
I don't want to get older I want to stay forever young, but I can't
I can't think about it
it just sucks
I want to be happy in the past but then again, I wasn't happy then
either
I miss the younger immature sadness
as we get older the sadness becomes much more complicated and
hurts more
I have nothing more to say, wait I do have to talk about good sadness
the sadness I have now sucks as it makes me mad
my rage builds I am just a rat in a cage Billy Corgan.
The world is a vampire sucking us all dry
It is somewhere else, and I am right here coping with my day to day
however, I can get by each hour, but it still sucks

one day at a time they say
why am I so mad why can't I be like everyone else?
I do not want to be at rage with oneself
I want to kill my body and demonic spirit but still be alive and happy
this would be a good thing I do think so I always talk to myself
I miss my friend Jeff, but our friendship is over we will never be the same
the more I age the less I care to feel
wait the more I age the more care about everything
I am truly ate up in the brain

LAVA LAMP

You never know what is good until its gone
You never know what's right until your wrong
You never understand why until you look at the sky
You never know what is true until you look within you

I DON'T KNOW

Think straight please as I do not feel
I can sedate my brain and become intoxicated until I believe
I believe in the ways of man
The man said go fuck you all
I will not know why it is I do believe
I believe I belong
I belong to know in my heart the song
I cannot believe if I can't think
I cannot think about nothing and everything at the same time
I do not know
go or stay and believe what you think
I think therefore I am to die, right or wrong?
To go as I can or cannot
I can't live in a world I don't know
I do not know

THE NEW NORMAL

Emotions! what crazy things?
mine are both obviously shown and yet put into all mighty cells withing my skull
here they thrive and build up until it is time to disconnect
to disconnect is to explode into an unanticipated panic attack
however, disconnecting does not work anymore
now I must have bigger colossal explosions to release my repressed anger
The rage deep rooted and disguised as pain
The pain is so happy when I am mad
my mind truly does not care about good and bad
the concept of good versus evil are so suddenly combined into a distorted array
This new distorted formation proves that neither good nor evil even matter
I think violence is now fun in heat of the moment
what others won't do I will
do I have enough guts to kill?
I hate myself that's for sure so I will take it out on everyone else around me
everyone will be responsible for my end result
nothing will ever be my fault and I will no longer do any wrongs
this is because everyone else is to blame
I am the product of my environment and the trusted persons responsible for raising me

I do hide these feelings very well inside
well with that sad
enough said now
I will do what I do every day which is pretend to me unbothered and
normal

NEUTRALIZE

I hate this and I hate everything
I wish I could have some pictures letters, videos, of my childhood
my life is an ongoing process of neutralizing depression, anger, resentment
the flashbacks and instability fill my mind with constant chaos
please feel your pain through me
I've felt enough pain now that I don't care if I have any more added on
my mind is absolutely blown in so many sections
the emotions, feelings, & responses are hate, love, happiness, lost memories, depression, anxiety these are the consistent mood swings
I go through regularly in a single day
I have lived this way for a long time
Only in the past year have I been able to recognize the symptoms
it has affected me in such a negative way
I do not wish to go on here
I want to go somewhere else and start a new life as a young baby
a child never have knowing such hurt
an infant who has all knowing joy of everything
I just want to go and cause a major disaster
an epic event of mass destruction
these newfound feelings of hate are uncontrolled
I try but I cannot stop them
These writings on paper help to capture these angst feelings

FATHOM

Death defied my abandoned life
Our Strife towards the umbilical knife
Ashes to dust and denial of trust
Figure it out and the end will come
Your beliefs are made up of lies
Through them all I you justify
Your insecurities and imagination
Left alone for the resurrection
The hate is stuck in my mind
Through the love I will survive
Your disposition my fathomed night
In your heaven we will reunite

FALL 1992

My childhood years were pretty bad ways
My parents kept fighting it lasted for days
when I was 12, we got a new house
along with this purchase my fathers' new spouse
the family was twisted for the next 2 years
my mother's pain reflected in tears
I tried to be that noble son
but my family problems had just begun
at age 14 my mother sent me away
for one year with a sister I had to stay
the angst, fear, emotions I had built
they stirred inside me with a side of guilt
Choosing my parent was my next big decision
a small kid like me had to envision
A future in a newly discovered family setting
maybe some of attention I had not been getting
I'm 19 now and I'd like to say
that being on my own is the only way
I learned by myself the way to be
I couldn't count on anyone but me
everyone I know has messed up my head
belief, hope, trust, love was what you all said
I'm home alone and I'm living alright
I have got my boys and my girl in spite
of feeling hollow, empty, unloved & not good
crying every week from things you should
the things you should have:

said to me, been with me
listened to me, stayed with me
loved me, held my hand
just done something for me
because the decisions you made were not the correct ones
the lessons I will be teaching when I have sons
my children will grow up in a different place
where family values do not wet their face
this I swear by the god above
I'll give me kids my best and all my love

A DAY IN THE LIFE

Hey all my life is a little pathetic and sad
I was born and raised the small town of Jasper
A true alcoholic in the making
A green useless mind easy for the taking
My family left me there alone and depressed
They killed my dreams or at least what was left
Hey kid! look ahead your future is near
Fuck them all and deny my fear
Yes, I tried to win but at what cost
I once I had hope but now its lost
I did believe but now I do not
I'll try again eh no I wont
Hey, why grow up this way?
I ask my inner self that everyday
I've never done no wrong never been to right
So, what did I do to deserve this life?
Now you've seen the way I live
What can I do if I can't forgive?
For those of you who care and those who don't
I will live for them or no I wont
I'll live for me

EXIT 19 (WRITTEN WHILE DRIVING ON INTERSTATE FROM A SHOW)

We all leave on the Days of past backflash
And we all dream on unsupervised deviant behaviors
When new life is gone
we will comeback 365 days alone
life's fair when are children play freely
happy in their current lack of choices
they have no worries and no responsibility
no fears and no ability to fake
all real, all original, all alone
dying young is true freedom
because you never have to grow old
Span drains and bleeds your innocence
Eons commence cold arid aging assex of a person

FAR FROM HOME

I always ask why when I look at the sky
It seems to know me and sees what I see
My life has been good but bad
And sometimes I do get sad
I feel so unreal and out of place
My mind is gone, and time takes my space
Awake lost at dawn
I do not know where I'll be
Or how it will affect me
I really do miss my past
It went by so incredibly fast
I'll never know if my futures slow
My family divided bye bye
Some to live and some to die
Openly I lost my mind
I wonder what they will find
My secrets hidden for years
Filled with hopes, dreams, and fears
It takes me back to when my parents went away
I was young and wondered where I'd stay
Then I found a family home with peers
And again, lost my fear
When with them I was great
But somehow still felt hate
I resorted to cigarettes and beer
And again, lost my fear
Its unimaginable and unfair

How in life it seems people care
But we are all so such busy beings
I still feel lost somewhere in translation
Far from your reality and my sanity

JASPER

Welcome to this little town
No one here ever gets down
It is a happy little state of mind
Fall into it and you'll find
The true self or fake peers
And how to hide all your fears
Welcome to hell
You are now stuck in this place
Just another stupid face
Got money you've got power
That is the way the system works
This prestigious place that always smirks

Abercrombie & Fitch is the ways to be
Follow the crowd and you will see
All the grace that comes to thee
Be yourself and you will not go far
Originality does not count at the bar
Open mind is a fatal sin
These emotions come from deep within
Forget these things if you wish to prosper
Willkommen to my hometown of jasper

DEAR JUSTIN,

I have only one question concerning why we should split up, why? I hear the words you say my brain understands them, but heart does not agree. For the past couple of weeks, it knew it would all end, but I didn't want to give up. It hurt like a bitch to wait by a phone that never seemed to ring but I did not and don't want to let go. Congratulations you won my heart much faster and more sincerely than anyone ever has and maybe ever will. I knew I really cared and trusted you all along ever before I admitted it. It feels so strange the way everything fell into place. I truthfully believe we could be happy together but what is stopping us is beyond my control. You have helped me so much I wish you would let me help you. Just try, those words are very meaningful words that no one else uses very often. I love them words they give me strength, but meaningful words mean nothing unless spoken by a sincere person. Exactly what a promise is until it becomes overused. There are so many things spilling out of my mind so damn much hurt. I was cautious waiting for your feelings to be fake I finally decided they were sincere and admitted to everyone that I really did care. It's crazy I quit describing I care unfortunately that is only half of what matters. I know this probably didn't accomplish anything, but I want you to know I am here for you now. I will try my damnedest to understand everything about you and I will always care. I can't say I will always be here for you though I will be but not like this.

Liebe Immer

Gina

P.S.
The stars will always hold the answers if only we would listen

DEAR GINA,

Go away and leave me here
I do not deserve you
I'm half the man I used to be
So, what am I supposed to do?
I do nothing for you
So, what good am I
You sacrifice your friends for me
And I do not even try
At first things were all good
But things are not always great
My image of you so clear and bright
But I'm only allowing fate
So, don't cry for me when I'm gone
Cause you never were that way
My head and heart still yearn for you
But I'm that star that fades away
So, I leave you now and I give up
Like I said I'd never do
Cause people change I so did I
And my love was never true

Liebe Immer

Justin

P.S. You deserve someone strong and deserving of your love. I am by
starlight Mellon collie and the infinite sadness

STUTTER HEAD

I'm Looking back in the past
I'm ashamed of my own pretty face
The things I've preached have all been untrue
While I sit here contemplating my space
The even existence of feeble minds is apparent
The Substance abuse is bi product of our licorice children
Map me out on my highway
To get off away from the pursuing kind
Run away from not knowing ignorance
The end of our life and time
Kick out the cold social dialect
Then Walk home another day
Freeze frame the signs of those who stand looking
Reflect my mirrors conception stain
Learn to battle the bipolar intestinal Rabie shots
What is this world coming to when he dies bravely?
Nothing more nothing less

Sincerely his lost years

Stutter Head

<u>WEDNESDAY OCT. 15</u> <u>1997 11:25 PM EST</u> <u>OUR LADY PEACE</u>

I do not understand the point of my existence
There is this contrast Deja vu I sense alongside constant paranoia
This world truly scares me
In the still of the night I read the clouds
I feel the setting and once again I say
I've felty this before
I know this feeling
This spiritual divine is a depressant
Imagine having flashbacks of early childhood
Then back forward up to adolescence
In a life that is already fucked up
Right now, the climate is cool cloudy
It is a beautiful night
It takes me back five years
Seriously what is up with that?
My mind controls all
Its exceedingly difficult to keep up with it
In closing these are my feelings on this very night

BREAKING UP IS HARD TO DO

First off, I am supposed to be a loser but really things are harder than I thought. I am a confused depressed teen with no concept of art. It really is easier to give up than it is to try. A lot of searching for excuses and reasons to leave and still we wonder why. The more I think about it the more answers I could have come up with. Good, bad, or indifferent it was an incredibly stressful decision to make. In the end it was just easier to walk away. All the smalls things added up and culminated triggers. I was already frail and bedazzled and could not cope with my everyday self. I felt very strongly for you and that truly scared the shit out of me. I could not put down the protective walls that shield my heart from the outside world. I have been hurt so many times by so many people that I care about. It was just a bad time in my life, and I could not risk it for the reward. I am sorry

1ST SONG AMATEUR BLUNDER (THE FAB RECORDING SESSIONS 1999)

I gave you all my trust & you gave me nothing in return
why we go round and round then you left me her on my own
to this day I do not understand to the rules to your game at hand
by myself is the way to be because I cannot count on anyone but me
life is a process of holding back to yourself
no, I cannot take it just come save me from myself
I do not understand the holding back to yourself
why I cannot take it because of myself
Life is a bitch holding back to yourself
I cannot take it save me from myself
I gave it all to you & you gave me nothing new
why we do this, and you leave me here on my own
I, I do not understand your thinking as I would have done it all for you
I do not understand why, why, why, why you had to put me through this
I gave you everything I had but it does not make a difference to you
why did you have to treat me this way I gave you all I had you gave me nothing back
I would give in to you even though the shit you put me through why, why, why you

ANGEL

When I place my hand in yours
it feels so good this love we hold
we meet as one
me and you
as one in dreams
I dream into you

GLIMMER IN THE HORIZON

So much for the promises you made
A better life a hand to hold
So long to the months we spent together
Seemed so great but now its old
There is a glimmer in the horizon
Where the sun does not seem to fade
It is here that I find happiness
Its unaffected by the shade
We shared adventures across the open plains
Walking talking waking in bed everyday
Questioning our pasts
The reasons things did not last
No conclusions came to mind
Our love is blind
At first you could not see
That in the end you would leave
The person the place
The time the space
The years left behind
When you realize this isn't what you wanted
You cannot press rewind

I LOVE YOU UNTIL
THE DAY I DIE

Hey Lady If, you just trusted me
You are over their smoking cigarettes
Trust me These things do hold true
An honest Kids laughter in the sun
My friends are not number one
Huh, My beer of choice
My answer with hesitance in my voice
To be cost effective with the upmost quality
The factors of objectivity
Ill rent a video for you from blockbuster
A romantic comedy that I'll watch with you
Our hours together are so much fun
I really do love you

PATRICK 2004

So peaceful so puzzled we lay ours down in defeat
A slow walk to the corner side
Across the smooth
The smooth pavement winds
Conversing on memories
The stories tell the truth of our lives
Were still wanting and wishing
To bring new meaning to out thrives
Were unscathed by encounters
To believe in the mystery of our power
Conversation of good times and memories Those golden days
Your hand so small it fits comfortably with mine
The missing piece to the puzzle that has been lost along the line
Ashes from the cigarettes blow rapid across your face
Self-harm destroying implement of disgrace
Yet unscathed by the encounter
A bright smile rises bringing new meaning
Faith for nothing
As nothing is ever perfect in a world run with hate
The simple people continue with aspiring fate
A source of power so great
fueled by the ignorance of evil
the eyes of innocence
she shines almost ideal
to perfection with you a great sense of self

SIN AGAINST

A kid barely survives in his lonely ways
He's trapped inside his episode and the mood won't fade
He's the product of antisocial behaviors trained by defense mechanism
People who do not believe in communication
They do not believe in sharing feelings
He has no way to escape the this dealt hand
And he screams
No one can hear him
He stands in one spot for days
Thinking of all the things he could say
Isolated & alone walking his solo path
Is this the final act
An end to the misery
Please it must end
To free himself
His physical form dead to the world
The false prophets will say
He sinned against one's own making
I just need to stop
Take a breath
Stop thinking and take one day at a time

STAR

Next step up and sink inside the hole you dig
The hole in which you lay
You feed off the vibe that has been forced upon you
All this embarrassment you try to hide
Jump back in son
Ride the bandwagon and hitch a ride
Slowly paced and little progression
A stalemate
No reason to move fast ahead
Forget the past
Live for the future
Live for yourself
Save the world lose the girl

AUGUST BURNS RED

All the way down
The undertow subsides
It makes an amends
The shadows fall
The babies cry
We are all so weary
The fear of becoming what you hate
I did right from the start
I'm living in vain
Living our parent's life
I am fighting myself
To understand the canvas
You must understand the concrete
Understand the stage
As august burns
Red and white fly
So, cared to fall behind
Learning for much more
Honest and forthcoming
How much longer
Will we sing
Will we cry
We can only separate the powers that divide
Understanding a car crash

WHAT CAN I DO?

How can you expect me to just walk away?
I have devoted so much time and I do love you
Everything we used to have still means something to me
I hear the words you say but I do not want to be free
I care about having that someone
A person so close that I know I can always count on
To be there right there no matter what has been said
I need to know that my inner light is not dead
I met you in the warm days of June
The temperature that weak did not heat me near as fast as you
To restore confidence in a hopeless soul like mine
And now you wonder why leaving me is not fine
Please try to understand how deeply this pains me
The past year has tested deep nerves you cannot see
I'm trying not to give up the goodness and the fight
This struggle within to succeed through the darkness each night
Please won't you stay a little while more
You can watch me take the extra time to prioritize and reconcile
My anxiety, anger, upset, stress, emotions of denial
To come right past
To shine right through
I ask you now
What can I do?
I

LOCKED INSIDE MY HEAD

I am sorry for the way I treated you
I have been mistaken in my actions
My deep insecurity shadowed in absolute doubt
Some please come save me from myself
I live life on the edge of a guilty ledge
I do sincerely apologize
I've been locked inside my own head
I Fall to the ground
Have you ever asked yourself?
What do you think of me?
I'm sure it wasn't the answer you were hoping for
The incidents I'm so ashamed of
Seem to rise above
Even the best thoughts with you
They Do not even add up
All the times I promised you the world
I did not mean to lie
Everything seemed in plain sight
It was never too far to try
Anything you could have asked for
It was all within your reach
I guess I lied to you again
I failed to honor my speech
So now you leave me here and I am all alone
Do you think I have what it takes?
To abandon your security throne
Hey kids, Hold them close right to your heart

I wish I would have called this out
Right from the start
Feelings I should but dint hide stand out now
The things you never said to me
Although I wanted to hear
I am trapped inside my own mind
I am Closed in and insecure
I feel helpless and trapped to the floor
Your open and wondering free
I hope your happy in your choices
Did you think before you made by me?
I have sat in the corner for days
There is no one around
Emptiness is all I hear
A room without a sound

MUSIC IS LIFE 4-12-1998

DEFTONES

KORN

SNOT

VISION OF DISORDER

LIMP BIZKIT

COAL CHAMBER

(HED)PE

SUGAR RAY

HANDSOME

TOOL

FAR

INCUBUS

SMASHING PUMPKINS

COLD

SPINESHANK

GREEN DAY

BAD RELIGION

THE OFFSPING

NADA SURF

STONE TEMPLE PILOTS

DRIVING IN A MIXED-UP WORLD

driving in a mixed-up world
my stomachs cramped and its curled
cause pain is my middle name
I still have never felt the shame
In wanting to be something
something more
I wanted to be something
something
But now I am nothing
I flew down in the neighborhood
The police think they could mess with me
Me and my only friend
They learned how to fight when I took my own right
I ran and ran because nobody knows what's it's like
To go out with a fight to be like me and nobody feels quite like me
because I am injured
I am injured
but I do not care

A SUMMERS NIGHT'S DREAM

I broke up with my girlfriend from jail
She pays several men to hurt me physically
They stab me in with a hypodermic needle in the chest
I suddenly freak out on a bad acid trip in Buehler's Buy Low parking lot
We move to a big party in Germantown's parking lot
I am freaking out hiding behind a shopping cart
I get pissed off the next day and storm into my EX-girlfriends' room
I slam her to the bed and yell at her until the NUN kicks me out
Saying we were having sex
I leave the room and run into a Lauren/Kristen mix of a girl
I told her I was pissed and really wanted to have sex
We go to a soccer game and make out under the bleachers
She is only wearing her underwear at this point
I slowly push my two fingers into her crouch
Suddenly my EX is sitting next to me
I then wake up to the damn phone

TEENAGE LOVE

I am confused and scared! I do want to be with her, but I do not feel like its mutual. It appears as though she wants me to break up with her. If I do break it off, she will not feel guilty for doing so. I really do want to be with her, but she does not seem as excited when we are together. She worries what her friends are doing, and this makes me feel so unimportant. When I want to do something, I do not feel like I am missing out on anything. She however does:(I try to let her be with her friends so that she will be happy. I just do not know. I feel like she is happier without me. When she is supposedly upset, she acts normal around others. I feel guilty for trying to bring her to my level. I am always wrong. I try but constantly fail.

VERSIONS ARE ENDLESS
(A CALL FOR HELP)

Locked up in a desolate hall
I am blistered in the glory of the moon
This one is just an imbecile
One more thought is all too many all to soon
I am erased in the oceans of your soul
You have forgotten all we stood for
Mistakes have been made
It is really a one-sided story
Full of everlasting opinions
Their versions are endless
I have been living on the dark side
Continually pushing everyone away
Rebuilding all these forts around
The strength of steel will hold them up
Mistakes have been made
It's really a one-sided story
Full of everlasting opinions
Their versions are endless

THE BEST TIME
OF MY LIFE

The summer of 1992 was the best time of my young life. During that summer I found out how great it was to truly be a kid. So many little factors aided to the abundant happiness of that sizzling summer. It was in those days that we did not have to worry much about anything. When I look back, I can remember the simple joys of cartoons, swimming, baseball, and drawing pictures. The summer our family took a pleasant vacation to Florida. I enjoyed the white sand, warm weather, and the salty blue ocean. Just the small things we all take for granted in everyday life. This was the small things I enjoyed and embraced at the time. The true freedom to be young and hopeful. A whole world of simple pleasures and exciting days lay ahead.

IMITATION POEM

Justin
Outgoing, Weird, Different, Happy
Brother of Shane
Loves his friends
Who Feels family is good?
Who Depends on friends?
Who Gives trust?
Who fears responsibility and priorities?
Who would love to leave town?
Resident of Ireland, Indiana
Leinenbach

EPITAPH

The body of Justin Leinenbach husband, father, brother, son, friend
Like a smile in a coffee shop
A love of youth and freedom
But never to be seen again
Never to be heard again
Only to be asleep in everlasting life
Born October 28, 1980
Died 20??

JUDDER FAV. QUOTES

You Never Know What's Good Until Its Gone

Life Is Like A Box Of Chocolates You Never Know What You're Going To Get

You Can Do Whatever You Want

Knowledge Is Power

The Easiest Things Are Not Always the Best

Time Is of The Essence

To Be or Not To Be That Is The Question

Man Belongs to The Earth The Earth Does Not Belong To Man

One Small Step for Man One Giant Leap For Mankind

I Have A Dream

Give Me Liberty or Give Me Death

The Grass Is Greener

Worrying Is Like A Rocking Chair It Gives You Something to Do But You're Not Going Anywhere

Any Questions Comments Fears or Insecurities?

YOULL HAVE THAT

IT IS WHAT IT IS

IGNORANCE IS BLISS

YOU CANT ALWAYS GET WHAT YOU WANT

CHEERS

II CAPTAIN

LIMITATIONS

Emotional expression through sound
So Empathetic and true
Keep your feet on the ground kid
This is the story of the boy
A quiet kid sitting in the classroom
Never done no wrong
Achieved Victory through non association
To Rejoice in the solitude
The elements of sound
Just find another term for contradiction
A soothing melody
A grand display in the horizon
Anointing Secular pathways
Sacred places of the heart
Influenced by one another
In search of the rewarding career
Media the public's view
Acceptance please
A taste of wealth
Advantage over disadvantage
Out of the ordinary or unusual
Sponsorship and support
Separation of power
Progression through unlearning
Compare and contrast
In terms of a purpose
The relation between religion

Complex Structure of simplicity
Materialistic values
A play on his words
All points to persuasion
The featured item of the day
A social movement to sway
So clean and pure
With Innocence and honesty
To foil the enemy's plan
My changes in mood
A Perfect disregard of others
A Variation from the original
An emphasis on understanding
Disarmed and disarrayed
By what is so bright
Will it go will it stay
This sweet and heavenly sight

JAN. 6 1999 PAXIL

What can I say it's been awhile since I have had to do this? I just took a Paxil **Paxil** (paroxetine) is an antidepressant that belongs to group of drugs called selective serotonin reuptake inhibitors (SSRIs). We should be good from here or not. Oh my, my biggest fears are exposed at the roots. I realize them but getting over them is the difficult part. I fear I am like my father. I bitch, get in angry mode and then kiss ass to makeup. That is completely wrong. I swear I will not let this happen because if I marry a girl under those conditions my kids are fucked. I now realize these things because of Abby. That girl is the door to my world. Tomorrow is our 6-month anniversary. I love her with all my heart but there is a certain flow to our relationship. First is the constant struggle over control of the relationship. I feel I consistently lose in this situation. I am a very jealous, overprotective, insecure and scared man. I immediately bring all problems to her attention. She has no complaints, and this brings me more confusion. It seems I am the only one complaining here. This brings me so much more guilt and just sinks me lower into depression. Another problem is in her inability to see small problems and the pain each cause. I am screwed either way my worries feed off anything and everything. All I want is just some simple stability in us and myself. I want to be my best for her but sometimes I feel the furthermost thing from that. I do not know? it's crazy and a bit sad. I am so whipped over her. I basically live on her every word. She makes and breaks me constantly and I cannot build the will power to do anything about it. I depend on her. This alone terrifies me because I hate trusting and depending on people. If you believe in someone else, you get let down. This is the way I have trained my brain. If you only trust yourself, you only have yourself to blame if things do not work out the way they were intended. However, I have fell hard on this one and now I must build my walls back up. Build them to the point where I can be safe again. On top of my wall I stare down at the hurt and loneliness as it prepares to ascend above. I stand above the pain below able to resist its torturous ways. I have been hurt and let down countless times and each additional time does not get easier. It just makes me try harder to avoid people and difficult situations. This is life and confronting danger is a necessary part of survival. We all must cope with some level of discomfort within ourselves and the outside world. Facing fears is always a difficult challenge but one we must do in order to reach a solution.

TRUST 6-6-1999

Alone, I put faith in you
You let me down
You are a Liar
That is all you are
Justify your reasons
You let me down again
I tried to believe you
It blew up in my face
I will never trust again
Thanks for your faith
You gave up on me again
What is new
Nothing to me
Your sins my wins
An ability to see
The flaws within me
My trust is my downfall
Love thee through true sacrifice
Pride and consciousness
I'll give in to you again

SEND ME AN ANGEL

Send me an angel
Or a devil in disguise
Whatever it takes to get out what is inside
The efforts are not there, and It is not that I don't care
Volunteer your shoulder and You will see a kid crying out
There is no love in my life, instead Only a lonely hole
A hole that I try to fill by abusing large quantities of drugs and alcohol
Wher4 does this void come from?
It makes the hours linger on and the simplest of accomplishments impossible
Have you ever wanted to sleep it all away?
To lay still and unawaken by the pain
This is not normal, and it is not right
My deteriorating heath
No strength h left to get up
Is it empathy or apathy?
Quit talking now
Leave me alone
These words fill the gaps on what should be silence
The mind-altering drugs
The substance abuse is the happiness
At the end of the bottle
I am just a burn out
A burnt-out excuse for being nothing

BELIEVE IT OR NOT
I'M HAPPY

Believe it or not I'm happy
Despite the awful things I write
Believe it or not I'm happy
Despite broken dreams I still have sight
To the things that I want
For the things that I need
My hope is Dwindling in the light
Believe it or not I'm happy
For the gift of this terrible life
The crying of my children
The yelling it's my shame
Shining smiles pierce straight into my eyes
Not knowing if we can afford
All the things I promise
The spare change in my pocket
Is it enough for our next meal?
Utilities, rent, gas, to go
Will I be able to make it to the next day of work?
The physical pain and the fatigue
The swelling of my arms
The cost of my cure
Hey, I'm living the American dream
We are Working for what we earn
Alive or just breathing
That is the major concern

Believe it or not I'm happy
My hands they crack and burn
I remind myself I should be happy
To even be able to write these words

APRIL 16 2005 KEEPING UP WITH THE JONES

The courage under fire
We are all victims in the rain
Sink or swim little ones
So, your life is not in vain
You need to make the payments
Your credit is a score
If you want to build the white picket fence
You will have to work more
These dreams you can reconcile
The burdens your partner comprehends
Be there for one another side by side
Until the moment it condescends

8-8-1998 4:05AM DUDE WHERE'S YOUR CAR

Sometimes the pain is too much to bear. The past meets the present in an unwilling love affair. There are things you can just not let go. They continually catch with you. The most emotionally strong folks are those that have seen and survived the most pain. It hurts so much when times are good, and all is going seemingly well. You think hey I'm alright and then smack. Your brain impulses show you how wrong you are. Words cannot describe mental illness pain. This pain is felt in every fragment of ones being. It is felt as pain, sad, pissed, disappointed confused, regressed, repressed, achy, paranoid, sorrow, regret, trust issues, love, lust, vex, discomfort. This is how I describe pain. Everything small snowball effects until it is a giant wave crashing down on me in time.

SUNDAY 6-6-1999

I'm alone once again
I've never had a good friend
There's no one here to come help me
My days struggle on so slowly
If I could kill off my fear
I'd ask you to throw me a lifeline dear
She does not care
she does not love
she does not feel a thing
she does not mind
she's not that kind
I can never win
why oh why do I try to carry on in it
because in my mind it will get better with time
to suffer in this sin

5-22-1999 1:04AM (ARRESTED FOR MINOR POSSESSION OF ALCOHOL)

My faith in you is so thin
My love for you a lustful sin
Trust is so often overused
My love for you easily abused
Self-Care lies in a mood swing
Thoughts of me an unwanted thing
I try so hard but always failed
I don't try at all that ship sailed
My hope is always shattered within
I try not to give up, but you cut me badly again
Why do I not give up?
Because I love you is why I don't give up
Here's to my final words as It doesn't change a thing
I'll go on my pathetic path and prosper when I sing

HEY BLACK HEART

Never once have I put alcohol before you
When I'm there it doesn't matter
When I'm not there it does
I'm tired of being taken advantage of
You only need me sometimes black heart
You do not know mental anguish
Your main objective was to get drunk to dull away
You completely forget about me
Everyone was asking where you went
I said she will come back once she's drunk
When you finally arrived, I was resentful
I wished your drunk ass would go away
Your friends and booze are more important than me
I receive extraordinarily little attention from you
I especially love the way you act serious for a second
The next moment is a complete laugh out loud
Saying sorry does not fix all problems
You must take responsibility for your actions

9-20-1999 (VINCENNES UNIVERSITY FRESHMAN YEAR) UNSPOKEN

Senseless spoken words raining down on a useless world
You are trying to call this place your home
It is
With no one to care and no thoughts of concern
A lonesome quest for identity and security in
an unfamiliar place that provides none
The purpose to this existence is not understood
Confusion leads to schizophrenia in the common minds of those who
stand looking
Their sights are often blinded by
the harsh reality of their unpredictable environment
Why is it that you want to live?
Do you want to live for better days and brighter nights?
Are you in a challenge for serenity that is beyond your control?

GIRLS

I love my life when I'm with you
You give me strength and courage
You bring joy to a dull evening
You make me laugh when I'm down
You hold my hand and my heart
I beg this never falls apart
You screwed it up again
I swear girls have a master plan
Guys will do anything for you
You screw us over through and through
I'm lying to myself
I hate you
I love you
I can't live without you

WAYNE 8-12-1998 1:39 AM

Hey dude
Differences between us add up all the time
These troubles and anguish injure us in our prime
Seems confusion and regret follow us all around
Conflict seems to hear our every sound
I really don't know why we are the way we are
The music soothes us though as we listen to FAR
We both have mental problems that stick with us like glue
We both really have no clue what will aid us through
Dude the way we feel is fairly bad
Both our pasts are pretty sad
Our future as friends is on the line
You take your road and I will take mine

WORDS TO LIVE
BY OR UNDER

LIMIT
DISPLACE
ACTION
BARRIERS
CONFINE
FRUSTRATION
STRENGHTH
RESTRICT
REGULATE
MOTIVATE
COLLIDE
DEBATE
EXIST
EXPRESS
TALK
SPEAK
SCREAM
DERIVE
CRUEL
DAMAGING
GUILT
INTENSE
REGRESS
REPRESS
CRUSHED

AGGRESSSION
DISGUISE
MANDATE
DEPEND
CHEMICAL

KILL THE LIGHT

Rape my mind
I'm always the victim
Nothing is wrong with me is there
Give me a sign
To break way
To say to her
I'll be ok
Break way my mind
Its lost in time
Held away by darkness
As skin creates black
Black, the color of my heart
Emptiness inside
Self-actualization shows me nothing
Basic needs I've never known
The roots to this seed have not grown
Unleash the chaos on me
Deal me the bad hand
Disaster is always
Feel this speak out
Loneliness is my companion
Fall down without a sound
Decline the memories
Emotions are steady
Escaping myself is retreat
Initiative is not there

No motivation to do anything
Lacking Pride
Call me a pussy and I won't deny
Deviance is not a solution

THE SCORCHED EARTH POLICY

The world is a crazy place
taking up my time and space
I hate it all it makes me mad
Mellon collie ever sad
Feel the rage all around
Coming from the underground
Break these chains that hold my remains
Forever in your heart
Now you've learned what's in the large vessels beneath my skin
Destroy your mind destroy all man
Think really hard and you can
Why can't people see all the hate inside of me
Now stop all sins cause in the end no one wins

NOW I TRY TO WRITE A SONG

Now I try to write a song
Love never lasts too long
Things are just a sudden urge
The important things you always purge
Items felt in the heart
Shoplifting at the local Kmart
Running through the summer sun
And in your mind your number one
It's called youth it went really fast
and that is why now it's called my past

BORN ON THE 4TH OF JULY

I feel sick
Life plays another trick
Ill hurt and somewhat confused
The outside world is so amused
Red white and blue
America colors surround you
Full of your own nations pride
Hear these words and try to hide
We all loved you number one
And you were our only son
Participation in his war
And now you are alive no more

HAPPY BIRTHDAY

Justin:

Your hard to buy for so I will just give you money

Happy Birthday

Love
Dad

4-21-1997 MISSED A DAY

These past few weeks have been very eventful for me. I have found something to care for & Someone to love for. Her name is Gina:) It is through her that I have found new things in Life. New feelings that I never would have cared for otherwise. Gina has confused me so much, but I confused myself so much more. It is this new hope and confidence in someone besides me. It brings me joy and security while tugging at my heart strings. This in turn causes my anxiety to flare up and my insecurity to be on full alert. My feelings of hate have gone into hiding for the past month. I'm am trying to be a better me. New events—reduce smoking, reevaluate my life and time management, learn to care about others, try to understand other people's feelings.

4-22-1997 FOUND A DAY

Ok, Today I try to quit smoking for the fiftieth time. I have so many things pushing me to quit right now so I might as well. I do know it's bad for me blah blah blah. Its bad but it holds me center. I do not care anymore… I quit, I quit, I quit. I'm doing this for me, myself, and I. (DAD, MOM, GINA, CHARLIE, AND THE REST OF THE WORLD) No more air pollution from me……..

MONDAY 8-11-1998
LIMP BITCHKIT

Here we again as today I write in the depression of happiness. Lately I have been discovering this happiness? Life is so fucked up. I can truly find happiness in the dumbest of places somedays and on other days it is nowhere to be found. It is this certain uncertainty and slap happy mentality that cripples and confuses me. But hey Life is easy right? The secret to this life is to take things as they (wait). I forget what I was going to say. Oh, shit I just lost the secret to life? WTF

OCTOBER 16, 1998
STRUGGLE BUS

Cliff Notes For A Teenage Relationship Struggle Week

She makes me feel bad and guilty
We are not on the same level
I would for you, but you wouldn't for me
I want things to be the same as before
I do not want to change
I am a bad guy
I'm sorry
I feel taken advantage of
Kelly Schue says this is normal
Ill try to not smoke
I love you
It's been three months
Ill get you a gift
I will get a haircut
I need to work on my ollie
Friday is date night
Saturday is partying with friends
When the next vacation to Florida
Meet Jamin at Loris

JUSTINS ROOM

You can continue to worry if you want to
Ask me if I care
This crazy world around us
is the reason for our despair
This life really is a process
You should continue to Follow it through
The evolving cycles of maturing
They Shall show you what to do
Listen if you may
If you really care about what I have to say
You will wake up in the morning & live another day

JULY 9, 1998 11:30PM

Dear Abby,

These fumbling words cannot describe
They way I truly feel inside
Imperfections, wrong doings, the things I try to hide
My insecurity, hopelessness, lack of faith
They must be ignored
I must change soon so that you do not become bored
Believe in me like I believe in you
Our new hope and good fortune will surely lead us through
What is often good but what can also be bad
All the new feelings and life experience that we never had
Until now we held hope's light at first
All the past mistakes & troubles we have cursed
Stay with me and I will be true
But No matter what I will always love you

Justin Michael Leinenbach

BULLET WITH JUDDERFLY WINGS

Your world is my empire
Sent down by rain
secret employers
hold you up for the games
and what do I get for going insane
frequent flyers
and a big great Dane
even though I flow
I suppose it'll snow
All my cruel and cold
I don't like my job
Despite all my rage
I am still just stuck on this page

THE EVERLASTING GAZE

Feel the rage inside of me
Fill the world with empathy
Go crazy and eat a pill
Feel the breeze on the window seal
Complain again to your pain
That you cannot abstain
How can we withstand the everlasting gaze?
It has a hold on you

DO YOU SEE WHAT I SEE?

I sense emotion like a bird across the ocean
The constant commotion of feeling pressures motion
I am told worrying makes you old
Fuck the world and all who is here
Let us go somewhere that is full of fear
Steal your soul's energy for yourself
the killer in me is the killer in
I have no smile to send to you
eat your brains and kill your friend
cause all in all we all have the same end

HEALTH CLASS FRESHMAN YEAR

I'm Thrown away
Leave me here
Stab me with your social spear
Kill me now
Kill me fast
Have Pac man eat my past
I don't care
I don't mind
What the hell will you find
Eat your life
Eat your head
Have weird dreams in your bed
We are here
We are there
We are absolutely everywhere
We don't want to be
Why can you not see
We hate you
All your friends do too
Society must burn
Hail violence
Solute hate
It's all fate
These Broken chains control Chemical imbalanced brains

7-15-1998 ANOTHER ANXIETY ATTACK ATTACK

Oh man I was wrong
I said something I did not mean
I am a liar
I do not trust you
I fear losing you
I need to distance myself
I am going to destroy us
Things have been to perfect
We have spent so much time together
I love it
Being with you makes me happy
I feel wanted
But fuck it
Fuck you
Go jump on somebody else
I give up
I cannot care
You never really have anyway
So, what's the point
What's it matter?
Go on
Leave me
Its over

P.S.
I knew all along you would do this

YOU ARE WISHED

Hey Babe,

I know there is nothing I can say or do to help with the pain but hang in there. I am always here to talk to. I miss our late-night talks. I've had a lot of great times with you. Whether it was those conversations or hanging out at the good ole skate place. (Getting you in the doghouse) You did a great job Friday night! The best of luck to you and your 4Fit band. You're a great friend and hopefully will be forever. So, remember me when you and your band become famous someday alright? While I know we are not as close as we used to be, we should talk again sometime soon. Hopefully ill get to see more of you this summer.

Well see you soon

Love ya always

Laura

A look at the stars
a touch of the hand
you are wished
whatever comforts you
you are wished
what brings peace to your heart

CHAIN LETTER

ME---
Anyways
I have been working all week and her and I have spoken like once on the phone. We saw each other Tuesday for an hour. Yesterday I was having a bad day and I just wanted to be with her for a half hour before work. This did not happen. She and I did not do anything or talk to all day. She had time to talk to Jeff Spellmeyer on the phone for a half hour last night. So needless to say, since she couldn't find time for me I'm being a little difficult today.
Please write back

RESPONSE---
That makes no sense to me. I don't want to say anything, but it was a bad on her part to talk to Jeff and not you. That is not right. I mean you do not have to talk on the phone a lot but when you tell her to visit you and she doesn't have time. She does not even have time to call you but talks to someone else that is not good. I'm not saying anything bad but...
I'm sorry Judder
Cheer up

3RD party—
Oh Judder,
I'm sorry she didn't go visit you at work but I wouldn't worry about it. It's not like she doesn't like you or anything. You are both whipped! I bet you'll be fine by tomorrow. Maybe you'll make up tonight

ME---

Yes, but that is not the point. First of all, I was fucking down and out yesterday. I really wanted to be with her at least for a little while. To most folks that's not a big deal but I felt sad & lonely. I was let down when she didn't come to see me. It sucked and it made my shitty day feel worse.

So in order to not be all whipped and happy go lucky. I am being like a normal douchey guy and ignoring her. We are not fighting but I may be purposely avoiding just a bit. I'm sorry Babe but I haven't got much time to talk. HA HA

Paybacks a bitch

DISTRESS SIGNALS
OVER THE AIR

Now I try to write in a period of distress
My mind is so clogged with feelings
It's like a stopped-up sink full of tears
I am a sad lonely desperate man
I have once again fell into the trap of love
2nd time through here
The feelings I have our similar to the ones with Gina
I feel I have learned a few things since my last encounter
Some of this new knowledge is essential for a successful relationship
Kristen Schulte, I feel could be a great spouse
She has so many good qualities
Smart, beautiful and most of all an open mind
An open mind to difference
I feel so strongly attached to ger right now
I do not like being separated
I find myself insanely jealous and insecure
I really want to tell her how I feel
I fear it's too soon
What if she does not feel the same way
If not now, then when
Time flies and things happen so quickly
I must try now
There may not be a later

Sincerely

JML

New years
Jan 1 1998

Spoken sober btw in Jenny Stallwood's basement

D.R.U.G.S.

Drugs are need drugs are good
While on them you think you could
Be a star in Hollywood
Feel the pressure
Feel the pain
Take your drugs and wash away
I am happy I am sad
While on drugs nothing makes me mad
I feel no reason to go and hate
All you need is to sedate
All the things you do not like
Dream of hitting them with a spike
To the arm or to the toe
Feel the heroin begin to flow

MAD MAD SAD

Farewell good night
last one out turns out the lights
run away from me
I'll let you know I'm real
I am real
I am unreal
Scary
Everyone is mad mad sad
Lost in the world
So, let me tell you this
I am someone you will never miss
Everyone is mad mad sad
Lost in their own world
There is nothing to say
that I have not felt already in this way
can you see your wrath?
I'm trapped in the underneath
Everyone is mad mad sad
Lost in their own world
got to hate
please don't go and hate

IVE GOT FRIENDS
IN LOW PLACES

Judder,

I know that I may just be a face in the crowd right now but that is ok and completely understandable. I just feel that I should let you know that I am here for you. You and I both know that we have had a few run ins but I don't hold grudges and you don't seem to either. Overall, we have been pretty good friends. I know I'm not a Jamin to you and that is fine. I do however think of you as once of my close friends. One of the few people I would do absolutely anything for. I can't imagine how difficult this all must be for you, but I hope that I along with all your other friends can make it a little easier for you. I keep asking myself "what can I do for Judder" & the only thing I can come up with is to be here for you. You can believe that I really am. You have a lot of great friends because of your awesome personality. Way to often we do not let our friends know how much they mean to us until something terrible happens and we all need to pull together. I apologize for never letting you know what a great person you are and never thanking you for being a friend to me. Judder you and I both know that we are uncertain of where our life may lead us. Please know that I am thankful for the time that you have already been there and a part of my life I am here for you today and always.

Love,

Kara

ABS

Babe,

I really do not know what to say. I was just sitting here in study hall thinking. I'm looking right over at you and feeling depressed because I just can't get up and walk over to you. Basically, I am just really missing you which is weird because I can see you visually. Its crazy right! We have been together now for 5 months and every day I am happy for that(or at least most of the time). Any other girl thus far would have been gone from my life. Who are we kidding maybe even 2, 3, or 4. You are still here:0 Abs, I love that! I love being with you. I love talking to you. I love hugging, holding, hand touching just everything with you. This relationship has treated me the best of both worlds. Every day I am thankful and just happy to be with you. I am happy I really mean it. Most of my previous relationships would not last this long. They never really got to this point of maturity and acceptance. I would lose interest and things would quickly unravel. I failed my partners but this one keeps me on my toes daily. I can always be sure of that with you. I want you to always know how things are with me. I never want to take this for granted. This to you I promise.

Love always

J

CHRONOLOGIC

12
When I was 12 I lived in a beautiful log house
I loved sports
I adored the USA Olympic dream team
13
My Mom, Brother, and I lived on 6th St.
I started stealing Shane's cigarettes and smoking in the park
I fell in LOVE with Green Day
Music soothed my savage soul
Green Day, STP, Gin Blossoms
I started stealing
I wanted to run away
14
I lived with my sister Angie across from KMART
I would steal CDs
I enjoyed The Offspring, Weezer, Hole, Dinosaur JR
I had a crush on Jenna Schuetter
The best parties that year were Amy Hochesang, Jason Craig,
Adam Gilley
I hung a lot with Jeff Jackson, Brandon Sandage, Jamin
Hochesang, Connor Dumas, Andy Lyon, Aaron Buechlein,
I had a fun scooter birthday party that year
I lived in the basement
I got drunk on Red Dog beer
I smoked Marlboros and Swisher sweets
My grandpa died
I smoked weed

15

I moved into an apartment with my DAD
I lived in the living room and slept on the couch
I hung out with same dude plus Ben Seibert & Matt Sheik
I got drunk on Seagrams and OJ
I cried for hours listening to Nirvana
I rode my Green day Scooter everywhere
I partied with my Brother and his friends at "The Fab"
I smoked a lot of weed
My friends Connor, Jamin, and I rolled joints with fruitaburst papers
I used to walk home from school
Andy L. robbed the concession stand of power aid and candy
I had a big crush on Elizabeth Guard
New friends Flucky, Calvin, Bart, Colemans, Doug
We went to the OMNI hotel in Indy to party
Semi state that year

I AM DEAD

Jerry smoked pot and he liked it a lot
With every hit a new idea or thought
Dreams and hopes brought about just like this
With more drugs the world was his
Fans and friends became a weeklong trend
While thoughts of caring began to end
Soon drugs and music were all that was there
And Jerry never did care
Everything was all right everything was ok
All he had to worry about was getting through the day
Past and present join to make him great
And all the non-dead heads laugh and hate
Jerry still loves life and feels he is ahead
And so, he shares his love with the Grateful Dead

by Justin Leinenbach

POSER

Come on be just like them
Go Kill yourself just for them
They are so much cooler than you
Skip real friends and do what they do
Always Follow the cooler crowd
Matchbox 20 is the new age sound
Social smoking will get you warmer
And now your just another poser

Your falling into the preppy trap
Abercrombie & Fitch is where it's at
MTV for you and me
Sports are the coolest scene
Just be like them

Go to the shopping mall
Daddy's credit card is good for all
Be a snob and discriminate
Show your closest friends this fantastic trait
They wont care they will follow you
Do what you say do what you do
Cause your just another poser

Your falling into the preppy trap
Abercrombie & Fitch is where it's at
MTV for you and me
Sports are the coolest scene
Just be like them

Walking down the city street
Sublime is the new heavy beat
You are getting into more music
But you do not even know the Lyric
Keep it up because your going nowhere fast
But who gives a fuck your latest trend will soon be past?
Be like them your just like them
your no good to yourself
your no good

1-7-1997 MY DARKEST DAYS

Please god save me from myself
My mind is the ultimate weapon
It is capable of inflicting great harm upon anyone or anything
It has unlimited ammunition and Is not partial to peace
It can place in the cross airs anyone or anything I unwillingly choose
In the past months, my mental health has been questionable
my mental strength has resonated in the form of furious anger
It is has grown to an almost a full potential
A mental nuclear timebomb so to speak
It is about ready to go off
As soon as the time is right
I will release All this built up atomic energy upon the world
The ultimate wrath will bring fury and hell fire to all
For now the wrath continues to swell within myself

4 PART COST VERSUS BENEFIT --1997

A life is not without death
Standby your love through all hardships
The antichrist superstar
Help your friends in any way
Is it 4:20 yet
I care for Her
Cancer?
I like Gina
Lightning
Are you with Christ or 666?
I want to be with her
I miss her when she is not around
Star child
I am confused
To be Happy Go lucky
I wish she liked me
Heart
I am sad without her
I do not wish to be alone
I want her to be happy
I care more about her than any other thing

THE END RESULT
ONLY GOD KNOWS

Why do you love me when I pit you through so much pain?
I do try to make you happy
I try to say the things you want me to say
I try to say the things you want to hear
I want to be the perfect image
Your perfect everything
So, you will noy hurt anymore
I want to be so strong for you
So, when the world crumbles down on you
I will not move

I will be your wall
When life turns dark
I will be your light
I try and it try but I fail
I'm constantly losing my own battle
A battle no one can win
We say we love each other
I know your happiness and laughter
They are but a nervous sweet relief
A relief from awkward and uncomfortable situations
Your worries and fears shine through
Your anger is just another
So many imperfections in me
I am seen but not heard
Your heartache and sorrow
It kills me to see you like this
I know I cause you pain
Why do you hurt
It is because of me
I want you to know that I hurt to
The thought of never being able to measure up
The fear of being incapable
I cannot fathom you worrying
I am here to hold you up
You leaving scares me to death
The thought of being alone
It hurts so much I cannot let you in
I will leave first to avoid the discomfort
When the pain comes it will be on me
You fight me
Your trying to tear down my walls
You want to know who I am
You want to know how I think
How I feel
Do you really want to get down to the core of me?
My fears, hopes, dreams, and inhibitions?

If I let you in will you hurt me
Will you be disappointed with the real me?
My continuous battle of being who I am
Who am I?
To face who I am
To accept who I am
To love myself
To not hurt anyone
Disappoint anyone
Let anyone down
I just give in to others without compromise
I cannot be me
The real me
the true me
to afraid to show them
to frightened to let anyone in
I do not look in the mirror
I do not like who I see staring back at me
All the personal flaws
An infinite ocean of imperfection
Why can't I just look away
Why can't I be the side everyone says they see
I look and do not see me
Those are my battles
My existence a war
To win at life
To choose death and defeat
The answer is our decision
The end result only god knows
Will I change?
I hope you stay to find out

YEARLY TOP LISTENS

1990- THE BEATLES, NEW KIDS ON THE BLOCK, PINK FLOYD, THE DOORS, REO SPEEDWAGON, TOM PETTY, THE BEACH BOYS, ELTON JOHN, THE WHO, AC/DC, METALLICA, ELVIS PRESLEY
1991-LED ZEPPELIN, RUSH, JOURNEY, CHICAGO, THE ROLLING STONES, CCR, DEEP PURPLE
1992-PEARL JAM, STP, U2, BOYS II MEN, ACE OF BASE, ARRESTED DEVELOPMENT, WHITNEY HOUSTON, JIMMY HENDRIX, BRYAN ADAMS, THE POLICE, MADONNA, MICHAEL JACKSON
1993-SMASHING PUMPKINS, COUNTING CROWS, GIN BLOSSOMS, RED HOT CHILI PEPPERS, ALICE IN CHAINS. MOTLEY CREW, BLIND MELON, NIRVANA, SOUL ASYLUM
1994- OFFSPRING, CRANBERRIES, GREEN DAY, REM, SHERYL CROW, BUSH, LIVE, VIOLENT FEMMES, SNOOP DOG, DR DRE, TOADIES, DINOSAUR JR. THE FLAMING LIPS
1995-NO DOUBT, RADIOHEAD, DESCENDENTS, BAD RELIGION, SPONGE, ALANIS MORISETTE, BETTER THAN EZRA, FILTER, HOLE, LETTERS TO CLEO, NINE INCH NAILS, PHISH, OASIS, GARBAGE, HOOTIE & THE BLOWFISH
1996-KORN, WEEZER, LOCAL H, NADA SURF, MARILYN MANSON, BECK, HELMET, MINSTRY, SAVAGE GARDEN, SOUNDGARDEN, TRIPPING DAISY, WHITE ZOMBIE, RAGE AGAINST THE MACHINE, BUTTHOLE SURFERS, SPACEHOG 1997-DEFTONES, TOOL, SILVERCHAIR, DAYINTHELIFE, HUM, EVERCLEAR, FOO FIGHTERS, PRICK, SNAPCASE, JEWEL, POP WILL EAT ITSELF, JANES ADDICTION
1998-LIMP BIZKIT, FAR, INCUBUS, COLD, HANDSOME, DRAIN STH, GRAVITY KILLS, HEDPE, SYSTEM OF A DOWN, SEVENDUST, SNOT,

VISION OF DISORDER, SARAH MCLACHLAN, DAVE MATTHEWS BAND, SEMISONIC

1999-STAIND, OUR LADY PEACE, SPINESHANK, ULTRAPANK, STABBING WESTWARD, EVE 6

2000-LINKIN PARK, GLASSJAW, TAPROOT, BLINK 182, SLIPKNOT, 311, HOOBASTANK, MUDVAYNE, OLEANDER, ORGY, PAPA ROACH, BEASTIE BOYS, SEO TAJI, EMINEM, COLDPLAY, MINUS, BOB MARLEY, PENNYWISE, THE SMITHS, POWERMAN 5000

2001-JIMMY EAT WORLD, DREDG, SHUN, EMIL BULLS, ONESIDEZERO, SHORTIE, DOWNSIDE (STRATA), LOST PROPHETS, AMBIONIC, SAVES THE DAY, THE JULIANA THEORY, NEW END ORIGINAL, BIG BLUE MONKEY, SUBLIME

2002- BOY HITS CAR, EVIL ENGINE #9, TRAPT, ABANDONED POOLS, AVRIL LAVIGNE, BLANK THEORY, FINCH, PULSE ULTRA, STUTTERFLY, SUPERHEIST, SWITCHED, TAKING BACK SUNDAY, DASHBOARD CONFESSIONAL, TRUST COMPANY, VAUX, UNEARTH, VENDETTA RED, HOT HOT HEAT, THE MARS VOLTA, AUDIOVENT, DAYSLIKETHESE, YESTERDAYS RISING

2003-THRICE, BRAND NEW, THURSDAY, FINGERTIGHT, KADDISFLY, EMANUEL, THE USED, MY VITRIOL, NONPOINT, QUEENS OF THE STONE AGE, RIVAL SCHOOLS, STORY OF THE YEAR, 30 SECONDS TO MARS, THE PIXIES, THE CURE, FACE TO FACE, TATU

2004-36 CRAZYFISTS, MY CHEMICAL ROMANCE, SPARTA, ZEBRAHEAD, INMEMORY, DEPSWA, ONELINEDRAWING, AT THE DRIVE IN, CHRONIC FUTURE, COHEED AND CAMBRIA, A SMALL VICTORY, SAOSIN, DAYS LIKE THESE, HOPESFALL, JAWBREAKER

2005-GRATITUDE, MIDTOWN, RISE AGAINST, THE SLEEPING, CAMPFIRE GIRLS, FUNERAL FOR A FRIEND, MOMENTS IN GRACE, MUTEMATH, OPEN HAND, PANIC AT THE DISCO, STRUNG OUT, THE GET UP KIDS

2006-AFI, CHEVELLE, ILL NINO, DEAD POETIC, ANBERLIN, ACCEPTANCE, BLINDSIDE

2007-SLIGHTLY STOOPID, DANCE GAVIN DANCE, HALIFAX, RED JUMPSUIT APARATUS, SHINY TOY GUNS, STRYLIGHT RUN, SILVERSUN PICKUPS

2008-EMAROSA, SENSES FAIL, BULLET FOR MY VALENTINE, PANTERA, 10 YEARS, FLYLEAF

2009-IN FLAMES, CALICO SYTEM, AUTHORITY ZERO, SCARY KIDS SCARING KIDS, ATREYU, THE HURT PROCESS, IT DIES TODAY, KILLSWITCH ENGAGE, MANCHESTER ORCHESTRA, PARAMORE

2010-UNDEROATH, SUNNY DAY REAL ESTATE, SUM 41, THE CLASH

2011-WOE IS ME, A DAY TO REMEMBER, SILVERSTEIN, THE WONDER YEARS

2012-ALKALINE TRIO, ABANDON ALL SHIPS, BREAKPOINT METHOD, JUST SURRENDER

2013-BRING ME THE HORIZON, ALAN WALKER, WE CAME AS ROMANS, MEMPHIS MAY FIRE

2014-ALEXISONFIRE, FOR ALL THOSE SLEEPING, FROM FIRST TO LAST, NECK DEEP

2015-FAILURE, FIGHTSTAR, MAKE ME FAMOUS, MAYDAY PARADE

CONCERT CALENDAR

Many Many shows missed in this list….

* = Headlining band

*Bush
-NO Doubt
-Goo Goo Dolls
Rupp Arena
Lexington, KY
April 4, 1996

*Smashing Pumpkins
Freedom Hall
Louisville, KY
October 29, 1996

*Smashing Pumpkins
-Fountains of Wayne
IU Assembly Hall
Bloomington, IN
January 18, 1997

*Stone Temple Pilots
-Cheap Trick
Roberts Stadium
April 18, 1997
Evansville, IN

Ozzfest 1997
Deer Creek
Indianapolis, IN
Main stage
*Black Sabbath
-Ozzy Osbourne
-Marilyn Manson (Added to the Bill on June 15)
-Pantera
-Type O Negative
-Fear Factory
-Machine Head
-Powerman 5000

2nd stage
-Coal Chamber
-Slo Burn
-Drain STH
-Downset.
-Neurosis
-Vision of Disorder

*Rage Against the Machine
-Wu tang Clan
-Atari Teenage Riot
Deer Creek
August 28, 1997
Indianapolis, IN

April 12, 1998
The Brewery
Louisville, KY
-Tinfed
*Deftones

*Limp Bizkit
-Cold
The Brewery
Louisville, KY
June 21, 1998

July 16, 1998 Ozzfest '98-
Deer Creek - Noblesville, IN
Second Stage Bands

-Life of Agony	-Kilgore
-Snot	-Incubus (played main)
-The Melvins	-Monster Voodoo Machines
-System of a Down	*Motorhead (2nd Stage)
-Ultraspank	

Main Stage Bands

-Coal Chamber	-Sevendust
-Soulfly	-Limp Bizkit
-Megadeth	*Tool

*Ozzy Osbourne

July 27, 1998-
The Brewery - Louisville, KY
-System of a Down

-Incubus
-Snot
*Soulfly

Family Values Tour
Market Square Arena
October 27, 1998
*Korn
-Rammstein
-Orgy
-Incubus
-Limp Bizkit

April 1, 1999 Rock is Dead Tour-
Louisville Gardens - Louisville, KY
-Videodrone
-Rob Zombie
*KoRn

*Fear Factory, The Toy Tiger
-System of a Down
-Spineshank
Louisville, KY
April 21, 1999

June 29, 1999 Ozzfest '99-
Deer Creek - Noblesville, IN
Second Stage Bands
-Drain S.T.H.   -Pushmonkey
-(hed) p.e.   -Static-X
-Puya   -Flashpoint
-Slipknot   -Apartment 26(played main stage)
*Fear Factory(2nd Stage)

Main Stage Bands

-Godsmack   -System of a Down
-Primus   -Slayer
-Deftones   *Rob Zombie

*Black Sabbath

July 10, 1999 Limptropolis Tour
Louisville Gardens - Louisville, KY
-Simon Says
-Staind
*Limp Bizkit

October 6, 1999 Family Values '99-
Market Square Arena - Indianapolis, IN
-Staind
-Crystal Method
-KoRn
-Filter
*Limp Bizkit

November 27, 1999 Gobblestock 3-
Louisville Gardens - Louisville, KY
-Dope
-Chevelle
-8 Stops 7
-Loudmouth
-Sevendust
*Days of the New

December 10, 1999-
Louisville Gardens - Louisville, KY
-Professional Murder Music
-Powerman 5000
*Kid Rock

March 19, 2000 Sick & Twisted Tour-
Conseco Fieldhouse - Indianapolis, IN
-Mindless Self Indulgence
-Staind
-Spike & Mike's Twisted Animation Show
*KoRn

May 7, 2000-
The Galaxy - St. Louis, MO
-Not Waving But Drowning
-Taproot
*Papa Roach

*Staind
-P.O.D.
Egyptian Room
June 20, 2000
Indianapolis, IN

*311
Murat Egyptian Room
Indianapolis, IN
November 8, 2000

June 20, 2000 MTV Return of the Rock-
Egyptian Room - Indianapolis, IN
-Crazy Town
-Dope
-P.O.D.
*Staind

August 2, 2000-
Rehearsal Studios - Indianapolis, IN
-Liquid Gang (cancelled)
-Ultraspank
*Project 86

August 8, 2000 Ozzfest '00-
Riverbend Music Center - Cincinnati, OH
Second Stage Bands
-Primer 55
-Pitchshifter
-Reveille
-Disturbed

-Deadlights
-Slaves on Dope
-Taproot
-Kittie

-Shuvel (played Main Stage)   *Soulfly

Main Stage Bands
-Apartment 26   -Queens of the Stone Age
-P.O.D.   -Methods of Mayhem
-Incubus   -Static-X
-Godsmack   *Pantera
                          *Ozzy Osbourne

August 10, 2000 Ozzfest '00-
Deer Creek - Noblesville, IN

Second Stage Bands
-Primer 55   -Deadlights
-Pitchshifter   -Slaves on Dope
-Reveille   -Taproot (played Main Stage)
-Disturbed   -Kittie
-Shuvel   *Soulfly

Main Stage Bands
-Apartment 26   -Queens of the Stone Age
-P.O.D.   -Methods of Mayhem
-Incubus   -Static-X
-Godsmack   *Pantera
*Ozzy Osbourne

August 14, 2000 Ozzfest '00-
Riverport Amphitheater - St. Louis, MO
Second Stage Bands
-Primer 55   -Deadlights
-Pitchshifter (played main stage)   -Slaves on Dope
-Reveille   -Taproot
-Disturbed   -Kittie
-Shuvel   *Soulfly

Main Stage Bands
-Apartment 26   -Queens of the Stone Age

-P.O.D.
-Incubus
-Godsmack
*Ozzy Osbourne

-Methods of Mayhem
-Static-X
*Pantera

October 7, 2000 Ridin' High Tour-Headliners – Louisville, KY
-Rehab
-Too Rude
-Linkin Park
-Corporate Avenger
*Kottonmouth Kings

November 9, 2000 Back to School- Free Schottenstein Center - Columbus, OH
-Taproot
-Incubus
*The Deftones

February 26, 2001-Egyptian Room - Indianapolis, IN
-Tinfed
-Alien Ant Farm
-Spineshank
*Orgy

June 12, 2001- Ozzfest 2001 Deer Creek - Noblesville, IN
Main stage
*Black Sabbath
-Marilyn Manson
-Slipknot
-Papa Roach
-Linkin Park
-Disturbed
-Crazy Town
-Black Label Society

2nd stage
*Mudvayne
-The Union Underground
-Taproot
-Systematic
-Nonpoint
-Drowning Pool
-Spineshank
-Hatebreed
-American Head Charge
-Slaves on Dope

June 18th, 2001- Ozzfest 2001
Riverport Amphitheater - St. Louis, MO
Main stage
*Black Sabbath
-Marilyn Manson
-Slipknot
-Papa Roach
-Linkin Park
-Disturbed
-Crazy Town
-Black Label Society

2nd stage
-Mudvayne
-The Union Underground
-Taproot
-Systematic
-Nonpoint
-Drowning Pool
-Spineshank
-Hatebreed
-American Head Charge
-Slaves on Dope

July 7, 2001- Are We There Yet?
Emerson Theater - Indianapolis, IN
-Spiritfall
-Haste
-Shun
*Paradox 44

July 12, 2001- Warped Tour 2001
Deer Creek - Noblesville, IN
-Alien Ant Farm
-311
-Rancid
-H20 -Less than Jake
-Sw1tched
-The Bouncing Souls
-AFI
-Good Charlotte
-and about 30 other bands

-Misfits
-Sum 41
-tod.
-The Ataris
-The Distillers
-Vandals
-Fenix TX
-Guttermouth

November 14th, 2001
Creepy Crawl - St. Louis, MO
-Handsome Devil
-Lostprophets
*Hoobastank

February 25th, 2002 -
Egyptian Room - Indianapolis, IN
-Mindless Self Indulgence
-Clutch
*System of a Down

March 7th, 2002 - Sno-Core 2002
Egyptian Room - Indianapolis, IN
-Fenix TX
-Earshot
-The Apex Theory

-Glassjaw
-Adema
*Alien Ant Farm

June 5th, 2002
The Void - Cincinnati, OH
-Coheed & Cambria
-Finch
*The Starting Line
June 25th, 2002-
Emerson Theater - Indianapolis, IN
-Piebald
-Glassjaw
*The Juliana Theory

July 11th, 2002-
Conseco Fieldhouse - Indianapolis, IN
-Deadsy
-Puddle of Mudd
*KoRn

July 25th, 2002 - Warped Tour 2002
Deer Creek - Noblesville, IN

-Thursday	-Mighty Mighty Bosstones	-Reel Big Fish
-NOFX	-Bad Religion	-Quarashi
-Vaux	-The Used	-Death By Stereo
-TheStart	-Skycamefalling	-Further Seems Forever
-Allister	-The Starting Line	-Finch
-Home Grown	-Vex Red	-AntiFlag

-about 30 other bands

August 13th, 2002 - Ozzfest 2002
Deer Creek - Noblesville, IN
<u>2nd Stage</u>
-Pulse Ultra   -Glassjaw

-Seether   -OTEP
-Sw1tched   -Mushroomhead
-Chevelle   -Lostprophets
-Apex Theory   -Meshuggah
-The Used   -Neurotica

Main Stage
-Ill Nino   -Black Label Society
-Adema   -Drowning Pool(last show, singer died 8/14/02)
-P.O.D   -Rob Zombie
*System of a Down   *Ozzy Osbourne

August 20th, 2002 -
40 Watt Club - Athens, GA
-Dredg
-Deadsy
*Taproot

August 21st, 2002 -
The Cotton Club - Atlanta, GA
-Dredg
-Deadsy
*Taproot

April 12th, 2003 –
Expo Five – Louisville, KY
-TheStart
-S.T.U.N
-Coheed and Cambria
*The Used

July 5th, 2003 – "Lollapalooza '03" -
Deer Creek – Noblesville, IN
2nd Stage
 - Fingertight   - Cave-In   - Campfire Girls
 - MC Supernatural   - Steve-O

Main Stage

- Rooney
- Jurassic 5
- Audioslave

- The Donnas
- Queens of the Stone Age
* Jane's Addiction

- The Distillers
- Incubus

*Taproot "The Take It! Tour"
-Adakain
-Dear Enemy
-Deadwater
Fri. May 1, 2009
Calumet Lake Pavillion
Jasper, IN

*The Red Chord
-Heavy Lies The Crown
-The Black Candle Mass
Sunset Hall
Fort Wayne, IN
July 13, 2010

*Deftones
-Baroness
-The Black Candle Mass
Expo Five
Louisville, KY
August 31, 2010

*The Sleeping
-The Hiatus Flux
-Within Cadence
-Of Wolves & Angels
OCT 19 2010
The Rewind
Bloomington, IN

*Thirty Seconds to Mars
-Neon Trees
-Nova Red
-Sacred Sorrow
-The Hiding
-The Black Candle Mass
Expo Five
Louisville, KY
October 28, 2010

*The Tony Danza Tapdance Extravaganza

-The Black CandleMass
Nov 22 2010
Rhino's
Bloomington, IN

*Conducting From The Grave
-Pariah
-The Hiatus Flux
-Here comes Tragedy
Dec. 18, 2010
Rhinos
Bloomington, IN

*Motionless in White
-Should This Armor Fail
-Drogba
Jan 14 2011
The Rewind
Bloomington, IN

*Legend
-Monsters
-Arched The Flood
January 17 2011
Rhino's

Bloomington, IN
*Destruction Of A Rose
-Should This Armor Fail
-The Hiatus Flux
Jan 18 2011
The Rewind
Bloomington, IN

Shai Hulud in 3D Tour
*Shai Hulud
-Close Your Eyes
-Monsters
-I The Breather
-Counterparts
Rhino's
February 8, 2011
Bloomington, IN

*Belie My Burial
-Locus Amoenus
-Drogba
-Here Comes Tragedy
Feb 11 2011
The Rewind
Bloomington, IN

*ICE NINE KILLS
-Where the sun meets the ocean
-Should This Armor Fail
-Arched The Flood
-Of Wolves & Angels
The Rewind
February 26, 2011
Bloomington, IN

*Listener
-Anti-swag Fiend Party
March 6, 2011
The Rewind
Bloomington, IN

*And Then There Were None
-The Hollywood Ten
-Arched The Flood
-Anti-swag Fiend Party
March 13, 2011
The Rewind
Bloomington, IN

*Sirens and Sailors
-Call Me The Patriot
The Rewind
Bloomington, IN
March 22, 2011

*JT Woodruff "Hawthorne Heights"
-Within Cadence
-Thorr Axe
-Adam Widmer
The Rewind
March 25, 2011
Bloomington, IN

*We Still Dream
-A Face For Radio
The Rewind
March 30, 2011
Bloomington, IN
*Gamma Pulse
-She has fashion vice
-Of wolves & angels

-Within cadence
-Anti swag fiend party
Rachael's Café
April 7, 2011

*Sovereign Strength "INRI Clothing Tour"
-The Burial
-Creations
-Stand Your Ground
-Drogba
Rhino's
Bloomington, IN
April 23, 2011

*Across the Sun
-DROGBA,
-Anti-Swag Fiend Party
-Adam Widmer
The Bishop
Bloomington, IN
April 26, 2011

*Belie My Burial
-Die Atlantic
-Venable
-Should This Armor Fail
The Rewind
Bloomington, IN
May 3, 2011

*LIONS TIGERS BEARS
-AFFIANCE
-LIFE ON REPEAT
May 4, 2011
Rachaels Cafe
Bloomington, IN

*I am The Messenger
-Should This Armor Fail
-The Hiatus Flux
-Pariah
-Drogba
Rachael's Café
May 6, 2011
Bloomington, IN

*The Murder and the Harlot
-Die Strong
-Silence
-Should This Armor Fail
The Rewind
Bloomington, IN
May 17, 2011

*For All Those Sleeping
-The Color Morale
-Close to Home \
-The Air I Breathe
-Should This Armor Fail
Rhino's
May 20, 2011
Bloomington, IN

*LIKE MOTHS TO FLAMES
-THE BROWNING
-YOUR MEMORIAL
-DELUSIONS
-Should This Armor Fail
-From Cities Above
June 4th 2011
Rachaels Cafe
Bloomington, IN

*For All Those Sleeping
-The Black Candle Mass
The Venue
Terre Haute, IN
June 11, 2011

*This Or The Apocalypse
-Deception of a ghost
-Venable
-We came from nowhere
-Locus Amoenus
June 21, 2011
Rachaels Café
Bloomington, IN

*I DECLARE WAR
-Should This Armor Fail
-Til Seas Run Dry
-Of Wolves & Angels
July 1 2011
Rachaels Cafe
Bloomington, IN

*Rookie of The Year
-Call Us Kings
-And By Love
July 21, 2011
Rachaels Cafe
Bloomington, IN

*The Burial
-Copernicus
-A Hero Remains
-Day Of Vengeance
-From Cities Above
-The Donner Party

Aug 4th 2011
Rachaels Cafe
Bloomington, IN

*Lazarus AD
-Thanasphere
-Til seas run dry
-Deschain
-Aug 5, 2011
Rachaels Cafe
Bloomington, IN

*Dr. Acula
-Of Wolves & Angels
-Should This Armor Fail
Sept 2 2011
Rachaels Cafe
Bloomington, IN

*Jonah Matranga
-Aaron Chandler
-Chris Learned
Rachael's Café
Bloomington, IN
October 28, 2011

*Hatebreed
-All That Remains
-Should This Armor Fail
-Patriarch
-Branded By Hate
-Day Of Ruin
-Cost Of Sin
Sever This Illusion
December 8th 2011
Expo Five
Louisville KY

*For Today
-A Skylit Drive
-Stick to Your Guns
-My Children My Bride
-Should This Armor Fail
Expo Five
Louisville, KY
April 1, 2012

*Sublime with Rome
IU Auditorium
Bloomington, IN
April 20, 2012

*Rise Against
The Lawn at White River State Park
Indianapolis, IN
May 4, 2012
*Coheed and Cambria
The Bluebird
Bloomington, IN
May 8, 2012

*Linkin Park
-Incubus
Klipsch Music Center
August 25, 2012
Indianapolis, IN

*Bayside
-Man Overboard
-Senses Fail
-Seaway
Mar 23, 2014
Ready Room
St. Louis, MO

*Brand New
-Egyptian Room – Old National Centre
July 6, 2014
Indianapolis, IN

*Senses Fail
The Day After
-Marina City
Emerson Theater
April 7, 2015
Indianapolis, IN

*Incubus
-Deftones
Farm Bureau Insurance Lawn at White River State Park
Indianapolis, IN
Sun, Jul. 26, 2015 06:30 PM

*Dustin Kensrue
Old National Centre
Indianapolis, IN
July 29, 2015

*Underoath
Rebirth Tour
The Orbit Room
Grand Rapids, MI
April 9, 2016

*My Morning Jacket
The Lawn at White River State Park
Indianapolis, IN
May 26, 2016

*Dashboard Confessional
-Taking Back Sunday
-Brand New

-Saosin
Farm Bureau Insurance Lawn at White River State Park
Indianapolis, IN
June 5, 2016

*Thrice
House of Blues
Chicago, IL
June 23, 2016

*Brand New
-Modest Mouse
DTE Energy Music Theatre
Clarkston, MI
Sun, Jul. 3, 2016

"Weird Al" Yankovic "The Mandatory World Tour"
Farm Bureau Insurance Lawn at White River State Park
Indianapolis, IN
Thu, Jul. 7, 2016

*Weezer
-Panic! At the Disco
Klipsch Music Center
Indianapolis, IN
July 12, 2016

*Sublime with Rome
-Dirty Heads
Farm Bureau Insurance Lawn at White River State Park
Indianapolis, IN
July 16, 2016

*Chevelle
-The Dead Deads
Mercury Ballroom
Louisville, KY
Tue, Sep. 13, 2016

*Deftones
Egyptian Room – Old National Centre
Indianapolis, IN
September 19, 2016

*Beck
IU Auditorium
Bloomington, IN
September 22, 2016

Louder than Life
Champion's Park - Louisville, KY
October 2, 2016

-Slipknot	-Disturbed	-Korn	-Alter Bridge
-Ghost	-Clutch	-Sevendust	-Pop Evil
-Biffy Clyro	-Parkway Drive	-Skillet	-Trivium
-Zakk Sabbath	-Kyng	-Skindred	-Adelitas Way
-Crobot	-Sabaton	-Smashing Satellites	

*Story of the Year
-Bayside
January 27, 2017
The Ready Room
St. Louis, MO

*Journey
Ford Center
Evansville, IN
Sat, Apr 01 2017

*Thursday
Bogart's
Cincinnati, OH
Sat, Apr 22 2017

*Jimmy Eat World
The Bluebird
May. 16, 2017
Bloomington, IN

*U2
-Beck
Joshua Tree Tour 2017
Jun 6, 2017
Papa John's Cardinal Stadium
Louisville, Kentucky

Revolution Radio Tour
*Green Day
-Against Me
Catfish and the Bottlemen
Klipsch Music Center
Indianapolis, IN
August 16, 2017

*Authority Zero
The Hi-Fi
Indianapolis, IN
September 3, 2017

*Modest Mouse
The Louisville Palace
Louisville, KY
October 3, 2017

*Queens of the Stone Age
Villains World Tour 2017
Murat Theatre – Old National Center
Indianapolis, IN
October 18, 2017
*Glassjaw
The Ready Room

St. Louis, MO
November 1, 2017

*Emery (The Question 10th Anniversary tour)
-The Red Jumpsuit Apparatus
-Hawthorne Heights
-Forevermore
-Hearts Like Lions
Friday Nov 20 2017
Indianapolis, IN

*Gin Blossoms
February 16, 2018
Buskirk-Chumley Theatre
Bloomington, IN

*Underoath
-Veil Of Maya
-Dance Gavin Dance
MAY 16 2018
Piere's Entertainment Center
Fort Wayne, IN

*Weezer
-Pixies
Ruoff Home Mortgage Music Center
Noblesville, IN
Sun, Jul 08 2018

*Foo Fighters "Concrete and Gold Tour"
-The Struts
Ruoff Music Center
Indianapolis, IN
July 26, 2018

*The Smashing Pumpkins
-Metric

Bankers Life Fieldhouse
Indianapolis, IN
August 17, 2018

*Descendents
Egyptian Room
Indianapolis, IN
August 26, 2018

*Local H
Pack Up the Cats Tour
The Hi-Fi
Indianapolis, IN
September 14, 2018

*Adam Sandler "100% Fresher"
-Rob Schneider
Wed • Feb 06 2019
The Louisville Palace presented by Cricket Wireless
Louisville, KY

*In Flames
-All That Remains
Wed • Feb 20 2019
Mercury Ballroom
Louisville, KY

*Bring Me The Horizon
MAY 15 2019
Egyptian Room at Old National Centre
Indianapolis, IN

*Jonah Matranga (Far / Onelinedrawing
-Nathan Gray (Boy Sets Fire)
The Citadel Music Hall
May 21, 2019
Indianapolis, IN

*Dead & Company
Ruoff Home Mortgage Music Center
June 12, 2019
Indianapolis, IN

*Third Eye Blind
-Jimmy Eat World
Summer Gods Tour 2019
Sunday, June 30, 2019
Farm Bureau Insurance Lawn at White River State Park
Indianapolis, IN

Rockstar Energy Drink DISRUPT Festival
Sunday, July 14, 2019
Ruoff Home Mortgage Music Center
Noblesville, IN
*The Used
-Thrice
-Circa Survive
-Sum 41
Atreyu

Second stage:
-Sleeping With Sirens
-Andy Black
-Memphis May Fire
-Trophy Eyes
-Juliet Summs
-Hyro The Hero

*Stabbing Westward
"Darkest Days"
The Citadel
July 27, 2019
Indianapolis, IN

*Authority Zero
-Meager Kings
Hi-Fi
Indianapolis, IN
October 12, 2019

*Jimmy Eat World
The Bluebird
Nov. 9, 2019
Bloomington, IN

*Powerman 5000
-Hed (PE)
-Adema
The Citadel Music Hall
Nov. 10, 2019
Indianapolis, IN

*Tool
Sat, Nov 2 2019
Bankers Life Fieldhouse
Indianapolis, IN

*Sponge
Fri, Nov 15 2019
8 Seconds Saloon
Indianapolis, IN

*The Beach Boys
Sat, Feb 29 • 2020
Brown County Music Center
Nashville, IN

COVID-19 Pandemic ---All remaining 2020 shows cancelled

*Alanis Morissette
w/special guest Garbage

- Liz Phair
Thu • Jul 16, 2020
Ruoff Music Center
Noblesville, IN

*Deftones "Summer Tour 2020"
-Gojira
-Poppy
Thursday, August 27, 2020
Lawn at White River State Park
Indianapolis, IN

*Phish
Sat • Aug. 8 • 2020
Ruoff Home Mortgage Music Center
Noblesville, IN

*Incubus
-311
Sat • Sep 5 • 2020
Ruoff Home Mortgage Music Center
Noblesville, IN

*Korn
-Faith No More
Sat • Sep 12, 2020
Ruoff Music Center
Noblesville, IN

THE END..

Printed in the United States
By Bookmasters